BEING A PROJECT LEADER

*Quick Guide
to Best Management Practices
and How You Can Excel
as a Successful
Project Manager*

© Copyright Ready Set Agile! 2020 - All rights reserved.

The content contained within this book may not be reproduced, duplicated, or transmitted without direct written permission from the author or the publisher except for the use of brief quotations in a book review. Under no circumstances will any blame or legal responsibility be held against the publisher, or author, for any damages, reparation, or monetary loss due to the information contained within this book. Either directly or indirectly. You are responsible for your own choices, actions, and results.

Legal Notice:
This book is copyright protected. This book is only for personal use. You cannot amend, distribute, sell, use, quote or paraphrase any part, or the content within this book, without the consent of the author or publisher except for the use of brief quotations in a book review.

Disclaimer notice:
Please note the information contained within this book is for educational and entertainment purposes only. All effort has been executed to present accurate, up to date, and reliable, complete information. No warranties of any kind are declared or implied. Readers acknowledge that the author is not engaging in the rendering of legal, financial, medical, or professional advice. The content within this book has been derived from various sources. Please consult a licensed professional before attempting any techniques outlined in this book.
By reading this book, the reader agrees that under no circumstances is the author responsible for any losses, direct or indirect, which are incurred as a result of the use of the information contained within this book, including, but not limited to,—errors, omissions, or inaccuracies

BEING A PROJECT LEADER

Quick Guide
to Best Management Practices
and How You Can Excel
as a Successful
Project Manager

2020

TABLE OF CONTENTS

- **7** — **INTRODUCTION**
- **13** — **CHAPTER 1** Introduction to Leadership
- **31** — **CHAPTER 2** Got a Problem?
- **47** — **CHAPTER 3** Fight! Learn to Love the Conflict You're In
- **61** — **CHAPTER 4** There Is No "I" in Team
- **81** — **CHAPTER 5** Put Me In, Coach, I'm Ready To Play
- **103** — **CHAPTER 6** Level Up Your Best
- **119** — **CHAPTER 7** Serve for Success
- **127** — **CHAPTER 8** What We Have Here Is a Failure to Communicate
- **141** — **CHAPTER 9** HECG Secret for Success
- **149** — **FINAL WORDS**
- **152** — **LEAVE A REVIEW**
- **153** — **MY OTHER BOOKS YOU WILL LOVE**
- **154** — **REFERENCES**
- **157** — **GLOSSARY AND ABBREVIATIONS**

INTRODUCTION

PROJECT managers are ultimately responsible for the success of their projects. They have to work with a variety of stakeholders, from team members to clients. Their technical skills have been honed from all their experiences on projects: estimating how long the project will take, what it will cost, and the necessary tasks and skills required to complete those tasks. By now, they've shown their capabilities as managers and are ready to go to the next level. Although technical skills and general management capabilities are required to become a successful project leader, they're not sufficient.

In my last book, *Being an Effective Project Manager*, I discussed briefly the difference between being a manager and being a leader. You, as an aspiring project manager, are ready to take that next step to become a sought-after *leader*, moving up from *management*. Yet being a leader involves several *soft* skills that will serve you well in any kind of leadership position in the modern world and in your personal life.

Many problems you've faced require the application of new capabilities, particularly in interpersonal relations. Maybe you're having difficulties with individual personalities on the team being unable to work well together, or you're seeing many conflicts within or between the team and the client.

Communicating well is a skill. Although everyone learns to talk when they're young, as you know, the business world requires more than the ability to have a conversation or tell others what to do. Communication is not just about talking *at* other people; it involves active listening to figure out what they are saying. It's about capturing where people are coming from and ensuring that you understand their message before trying to impart yours.

Fortunately, you can develop communication abilities and improve your conflict management skills. Although the topic of managing disputes rationally is often not taught in schools, it's especially critical for project managers whose job is to manage competing demands from a variety of groups with different goals.

On the other hand, perhaps you're having difficulties with your team members delivering the project on time and budget. You're under a lot of unrelenting pressure from stakeholders to meet deadlines or add in extras beyond the initial scope. You may have struggled to get what you wanted from stakeholders. Thus, negotiation is another crucial skill for project managers that you can apply in all other areas of life, and it too can be learned and practiced.

Maybe you feel like you're being accused of things that are well outside your control. As a project manager, you know that you're the one ultimately accountable, yet external issues occur, and not all of them are preventable. Nonetheless, your performance is negatively affected anyway.

These are common issues for project managers. The good news is that not only are there known solutions to these problems, but most of them can be learned and developed with time and experience. Some people may innately seem able to find the solutions on their own, but for the rest of us, practice and dedication to improving will get us there.

In even better news, *the solutions you need are in this book*. You'll learn practical steps for tackling the issues you're facing and effective ways to improve your game. Becoming a mature project manager by developing your leadership abilities has obvious benefits for you personally. You'll no longer be feeling like you're rolling a heavy boulder up a steep hill because, once you can apply these solutions, you'll find your work has become fun, engaging, and rewarding again.

As a project manager *rock star*, you'll have the pick of opportunities because everyone wants to work with a PM that gets things done and plays well with others. Not only will lucrative clients want to hire you, but star team members will want to be part of your team. You'll feel less pressure and stress. Part of being a great leader is the ability to find win-win solutions that may not be obvious at first glance. Once you develop your talent for this, you'll discover whole new worlds opening up for your dream career.

You probably already know that *leadership* isn't only about the leader; it takes into account their followers too. There are benefits to others when you have developed yourself into a true leader. Stakeholders will find their expectations met or exceeded and the project delivered on time and budget. Also, developing the talents of those who work for you will help them level up their own skills and feel confident in taking on new challenges and responsibilities.

At this point, you may be wondering what qualifies me to provide all this information about the leadership in project management. I've been a project manager myself, for many different companies, and on various projects—from small to large and simple to complex. As I developed my skills, I discovered that the next level up was in improving my leadership skills. I've seen many leaders—both PMs and otherwise—succeed and fail, and I've captured those lessons for you.

I want to help PMs at any stage in their careers level up and become leaders, not just managers. The more leaders the profession has, the better off our clients and we will be. I'm sharing my knowledge in this book, so you can learn from past experiences and become the best project leader that you can be. Everyone has enormous leadership potential within themselves, including you.

In this book, we'll discuss what leadership looks like in the modern world and the critical nature of interpersonal relationships. You'll learn how to improve your problem-solving skills—including leveraging politics—to make your projects better. You will also discover how to manage conflicts and the necessary step to build and manage a successful project team.

You'll also learn how to develop your team members personally and delegate tasks to them without hesitation. This book contains excellent tips on how to achieve more from negotiations and facilitate productive meetings. As a bonus, I introduce the idea of servant leadership, with emphasis on listening, empathy, and emotional intelligence.

You'll discover better ways to deal with stakeholders, set expectations, and use your influence and persuasion powers. In the last chapter, we will uncover four critical capabilities hidden behind the abbreviation of HECG, which are game changers in today's world.

Does this sound great? I am sure you have developed certain technical skills and leadership capabilities during your career. But maybe you feel like you're missing something, or perhaps the fun has disappeared out of a job? Why wait to turn that around and lose this opportunity?

If you want to become a unique project leader, go ahead and get started on this book. *Become the leader of your dreams!*

INTRODUCTION TO LEADERSHIP

YOU'VE probably heard and read a lot about leadership, especially if you're already a project manager (PM). What does it mean exactly, and how does it translate to being a PM? In my previous book, *Being an Effective Project Manager*, we discussed the difference between a "manager" and a "leader." Managers focus on the tactical aspects of the project; leaders focus on the strategic.

Although your title is project manager, you are a *project leader* too. The more you can develop your authority as a project leader, the more capable you'll be of implementing complex projects, and the more people will want to work with you.

Leadership in a Nutshell

Leadership is a combination of skills, characteristics, and behaviors. Everyone has a distinct style. The good news is that wherever you perceive your leadership abilities to be right now, you can develop them further through training, good coaching and role models, and the desire to improve continuously.

As a PM, you have to master several technical skills, such as managing the scope of a project. You need to budget appropriately and communicate well with your team and stakeholders. Building relationships at all levels of the client's management hierarchy is necessary to generate a win. You should have a good knowledge of the tasks required to successfully complete the project and develop a schedule that doesn't tax your resources unnecessarily while still satisfying the client.

In addition—and probably most importantly—you must be able to lead your team and not just manage it. You need to influence your team members to do their jobs to the best of their abilities. You'll need to develop some leadership capabilities in addition to your technical skills that will make you a sought-after PM.

Project Manager as CEO

When thinking about project leadership, consider yourself the Chief Executive Officer (CEO) of your project. You're the one who would be ultimately accountable for its success, just as the CEO is responsible when the business starts going in the wrong direction.

The CEO sets the vision and direction for the business. They aren't the ones organizing employee schedules and assigning tasks. Similarly—and especially when you're working on agile projects—you will let the team members figure out how to get the work done according to schedule and leverage each member's strengths for the better.

Successful CEOs differ from their less successful counterparts in nine key areas of leadership capability (Stamoulis, n.d.)[1] These areas fit the strengths that a project manager needs to command a successful project.

1. Taking calculated risks

Playing it safe won't allow you or your team to grow. On the other hand, great leaders don't take unnecessary risks or act carelessly.

As a project manager, you must make decisions with imperfect information. However, you have to take the time to gather enough data and consider the consequences before moving forward.

2. Thinking ahead

CEOs are often compared to being a ship's captain. Poor managers and team members tend to focus on what's right in front of them. Imagine how quickly you'd run into trouble if you were only viewing the sea right in front of you.

Instead, looking far ahead will help you spot the icebergs early, so you can have time to steer around them. You must be the one scanning the horizon to spot those icebergs.

3. Thoughtful bias toward action

People who ruminate or analyze carefully are often helpful to the team. However, the executive needs to be focused on the actions to take.

Good leaders aren't taking action just to do something; they're taking action based on a thoughtful reason. If there's a rationale for the action, they will take it.

4. Optimistic

Henry Ford said, "Whether you think you can, or you think you can't, you're right." To stay optimistic and keep the team motivated, the leader must believe that the task can be done. They must also be the lookout for new opportunities and pursue them when it makes sense to do so.

5. Tough and tender

An old saying specific to project management is that if everyone's angry with you, you've done your job. You can't please everyone, so don't waste your time trying. A great leader will make unpopular decisions because they're looking ahead where the others aren't. They've spotted new opportunities, which means that people will need to change something, though most people don't like change.

A thick skin is necessary for your leadership as a PM, so you can let these comments roll off your back. You keep going, even after your team members have expressed their displeasure.

At the same time, you're not insensitive. Great executives don't just demand a change of their workers but help them adjust. They acknowledge when people are having a difficult time and don't seek to enforce their ideas through power or coercion. Instead, they influence and persuade. Finally, they distinguish between resistance to change and valid arguments and promote team members who come with better ideas than their own.

6. Emotional intelligence (EQ)

Later in the book, we'll go into more detail about EQ for leaders. For now, it's essential to know that top CEOs understand and can manage their emotions effectively. They display their feelings and don't bottle them up. At the same time, they don't allow their emotions to overwhelm their reason or affect their team negatively.

7. Ability to read people well

Being able to read people means that you have developed emotional intelligence. As a leader, you want to understand the various perspectives that people from different backgrounds bring to their work and how to combine and support them optimally.

8. Pragmatically inclusive

As a PM, you already know that you don't know everything, and that other people's viewpoints can be extremely valuable. You will need to make many decisions, and the smart thing to do will be to get feedback from other people.

However, you still need to make the decision yourself. Just because most people you speak to think that option A is correct, they could still be wrong. If you are sure that option B is right, you need to choose it, even though you're alone in your opinion.

9. Trusting within reason

CEOs need to be comfortable with a variety of people with a wide range of backgrounds and experiences. As a project manager, your team will include members with various experiences and skills.

"Trust, but verify." —Russian proverb[2]

You will often be in a position to hire your team members, and if you've worked with them before, you will probably have a higher level of trust in them. On the other hand, just like a CEO, you cannot trust everyone you work with blindly.

The Changing Face of Leadership

You might have noticed that many of the preceding leadership skills are interpersonal. Today's CEOs don't throw their weight around the way they may have done so back in the last century. Now, when business leaders misbehave, they're often frowned upon by the wider community.

Today's leaders have discovered the power of emotional intelligence (EQ) in their work. Unlike IQ, which has standardized tests and measures cognitive thought, EQ is the measure of interpersonal intelligence. There are three basic EQ skills involved (Psychology Today, n.d.)[3]:

1. Recognize your own emotions (self-awareness)
2. Manage the emotions (self-regulation)
3. Help others to manage their emotions (social awareness)

Fortunately, unlike IQ, which is largely fixed, there are ways to develop your EQ. You don't have to practice these tips at work only, but in your personal life as well.

- **Practice naming your emotions**

    For those who are already tuned into their feelings, this tip may not be as difficult as it is for other people. When you recognize that you just don't feel quite right, try to name the emotion you're having. Boredom? Frustration? Anger? Irritation? Be as specific as you can.

    Also, try to note what the trigger was. Were you in a situation where you didn't feel like you were in control? Was there feedback you didn't want to hear?

- **Ask what others think about your EQ**

    Speaking of something you may not want to hear, ask friends, family, and colleagues for their impression of your emotional intelligence. Where do they think you're lacking? Remember not to shoot the messenger—you need them to be honest, so you can identify the spots you want to improve.

- **Read novels**

    Sometimes people in business read only nonfiction if they read at all. They will often read biographies of successful people, inspirational material to stay motivated, or educational books. Nonfiction is important, but add in some novels and fictional literature.

    They allow you to literally step into someone else's shoes and live their life. It's a great way to develop the empathy you need to be an emotionally intelligent leader.

- **Manage stress**

    This skill is vital for all project managers, and not just the ones seeking to increase their EQ! PMs must juggle many tasks and concepts themselves while handling team members and stakeholders. It can be exhausting and lead to burnout. It also makes you irritable and less likely to communicate in an emotionally intelligent way with others.

    You probably know the basics already: enough sleep, nutritious food, exercise, and mindfulness practices.

    If you have a hard time sleeping, make sure your room is cool and dark, and shut down screens well before going to bed; not five minutes—more like an hour, so the blue light emitted doesn't interfere with your circadian rhythm. You can use that time to read your novel and help you be more empathetic.

    Were you having a tough time with exercise? Maybe your daily "stand-up" meeting should be a daily "walking" meeting instead, especially if you and the team can get outside to do it. Don't skip this vital step of getting your body in motion because it does increase your productivity and boosts your mood.

Leader as Visionary

One of the most critical roles that a commander has is being a visionary. CEOs create the vision so the entire crew can be on board and everyone can work to achieve the same mission—all row in the same direction. The captain sets the course by which the ship will sail.

Yet, there's more to successfully reaching the destination than just having the vision. The captain has to motivate the crew to do their best and keep rowing in the right direction. To maximize resources in terms of human capital, the captain needs to understand what drives them.

Also, the captain is the one who would coach the crew. Ship captains typically started as crew members, just as many project managers started out belowdecks as team members. Therefore, they're in the perfect position to work with individual members on improving their craft and skills. If the crew members don't know how to do their job properly, the ship won't reach its destination. Highly qualified crew members want to improve themselves, and good captains know that the more skills the crew has, the more likely they will be to succeed.

To achieve their goal, the captain must also ensure that the crew has the resources it needs. On a more grand ship, like a Viking ship or frigate, they would need oars, food, time off, and sleeping quarters, among other things.

On land in a project, team members need slightly different resources, but the PM must still ensure they have what they need in terms of materials and resources. Some projects might get by with a whiteboard and enough laptops for everyone; whereas others may require more. The project manager won't usually be the one going out to the office supply store to pick up some dry erase markers, but they would ensure the job gets done.

Captains are also responsible for problem solving on a higher level. Later in the book, we'll delve into this topic more deeply. Fundamentally, the captain's vision should not only set the course, but also look ahead for potential icebergs or other obstacles that could impede the ship's safe passage. When such problems are encountered, the captain has to figure out how to deal with them.

Likewise, the project manager must be on the lookout for hurdles that could block the team's progress and determine how to avoid or mitigate them. Problems could arise from communication issues with the client, natural disasters, or other external issues. To ensure that the team can complete the project successfully, the PM must clear away any obstacles or plan to move around them.

To win, they must be proactive. Captains don't wait until the ship is a few yards away from an iceberg to plot the course around it. Similarly, when a hurdle appears on a project, the project manager needs to solve the problem sooner rather than later, instead of allowing the molehill to grow to a mountain's size. Recall that great leaders are biased toward action.

Interpersonal Capabilities

Communicating, coaching, and dealing with stakeholders and clients—a project manager needs to possess excellent interpersonal skills to deliver successful projects consistently. There are a handful of abilities that PMs should stay on top of.

- **Communication (verbal and nonverbal)**

    Studies have found that most of a speaker's message is not in the words that they use, but in their voice and body language (Nguyen, 2014).[4] Although it's obviously essential to get the words right, it's even more critical to make sure that your tone of voice, speed of speech, and body language are supporting what you want to say—not working against it.

Imagine that you are speaking to someone who is standing in front of you with their head down and arms crossed over their chest. After you're done, in monotone, they tell you that they really enjoyed what you had to say. Would you believe them? Of course not: they seem defensive and disinterested.

Positive body language is constructive. When you're standing up talking to someone, make sure you point your body toward them, including your feet. Make eye contact, though be careful not to be creepy or appear too intense. Stay relaxed with your hands at your sides without fidgeting; however, you may use hand gestures to support your points.

- **Active listening**

Have you ever been talking to someone, and the instant you take a breath, they jump in, and it's obvious they were just waiting for you to finish so they could make their point? Or maybe you were the one nodding your head impatiently and hoping the other would hurry up and finish so you could speak.

By contrast, active listening is when you absorb what the speaker is saying thoroughly, retain it, and respond appropriately. This would require you to pay attention to what they're saying—not what their speech sparks in you or the funny anecdote you have about a similar situation. Also, you shouldn't judge nor dismiss what they're saying. What they're talking about may be new or strange to you, making it even more crucial that you not judge, so you can truly understand their message.

You may want to repeat back some of what you heard to clarify or summarize what you got from their speech. This shows the other person that you were listening to and understand exactly what they're saying. Likewise, it could voice how you don't, and they can explain it again.

Active listening helps ensure there are no misunderstandings or miscommunication. It also puts people at ease and shows that their needs are important too. This often becomes essential when you're de-escalating conflict, as we'll get into later in the book.

- **Assertiveness**

Sometimes people confuse assertiveness with aggressiveness, but they are different attitudes.

Aggressive people run roughshod over others. Such a manager would be more likely to tell their followers what to do while not allowing any questions or concerns to surface.

By contrast, a commander needs to be *assertive*. These leaders are direct and honest about what they want. They stand up for themselves, but without making other people feel bullied or disrespected. They're not accusing other people of doing something wrong, and they often use "I" statements.

For example, rather than telling a client, "You didn't get me the materials I requested," they might say something like, "I haven't yet received the materials. Do you know when I can expect them to be delivered?"

- **Self-confidence**

To advocate for yourself and your team members, you need to trust in your abilities and judgment while believing that you are worthy. If you have a lot of self-doubts or are too self-critical, you won't be able to make the hard decisions required of a *successful* project manager. You have to be able to think independently, which means that you have confidence in your thoughts even when others seem to be thinking differently.

When you're self-confident, you're able to admit to your own mistakes, because you know that being human doesn't make you a bad person. This allows other people to bond with you because you're not pretending to be perfect.

You're more willing to take calculated risks when you're confident in your decision-making. You know that you've weighed the pros and cons and can make a choice, even with imperfect information.

People want to (literally) follow the leader. They don't want to follow someone who acts like they don't know what they're doing, or appear nervous or unsure. This is why so many con men are successful—such people act confidently, and others are taken in.

As a project manager, creating an atmosphere of confidence encourages not only your team but also the client. They don't want to hand over the reins on something that could cost thousands—if not millions—of dollars to someone who doesn't know what they're doing.

Upgrade Your Interpersonal Behavior

How do you think you rate on the previous skills? Are there areas where you believe you need to improve? Fortunately, just as you can improve your EQ (which is the foundation of interpersonal skills), you can also get better with your interpersonal capabilities. Most of these can be practiced at home and in business. You'll have ample opportunity to become better at building relationships, which is critical to success as a leader.

- **Act with personal integrity**

    Stand up for what you believe in and question when others ask you to do something that goes against the company's or your core values. Whether you're at home or work, make sure you're aligned with what's important to you. Others will see that you stick to your principles and deliver what you promise, and they can build their trust in you.

- **Manage agreement**

    Managing conflict is a crucial component in leading a successful project, so I've devoted a chapter to it later. However, I'm mentioning it here because managing agreement is vital for interpersonal skills. Here, you would help people build trust and learn to collaborate. Providing constructive feedback will help maintain the agreement while allowing you to deal with difficult situations before they grow into mountains.

    You can practice this by looking for agreements whenever you're talking to other people, especially during conversations where views differ.

- **Reduce or remove distractions**

    It's hard to listen actively to others when your phone vibrates and buzzes with social media or email notifications. Turn them off, or, better yet, disable them entirely. Put your phone face down on a nearby table or counter, so you can't see your screen. Doing all this will help you pay attention to the person you're listening to.

- **Allow silence to happen**

    Some people are uncomfortable with silence and will rush to fill it with words. However, sometimes, not talking is the appropriate response if you've been listening because you may need time to put your thoughts in order. You don't have to babble while you do so; silence doesn't have to be bad, so let it happen when it fits.

- **Don't make others feel accused or wrong**

  When you're standing up for yourself, it's important not to do so by putting others down. Practice using "I" statements and not accusing others with "You didn't," "You should have," or any other kinds of blaming or accusation statements.

  If there are issues with other people, you cannot ignore them because that's how molehills grow. You can discuss them and stand up for yourself by being direct and explaining what you need.

  Obviously, this one works well at home too. Stop accusing your spouse or children and see how much more cooperative they become. Practicing this type of assertiveness will serve you well in all aspects of life.

- **Set boundaries**

  Just as you must ask for what you need, it's important to set boundaries, so people know when they're overstepping. Enforce them too, so others aren't demanding too much of your time and energy.

  I had a boss that would try to get the most out of his employees for what he paid us. You could end up working all night to finish something under his leadership. But I discovered that he was perfectly fine with boundaries. If you told him that you needed to go home to spend time with your pets/kids/spouse and work on it the next day, he was okay with that.

  I don't think he meant it maliciously; I just had to let him know that he couldn't expect me to work late every night when I could get things done on time. There were times when I did need to work late to finish, and I didn't resent it thanks to the boundaries I had set.

- **Fake it 'til you make it**

    This approach does not work for project managers most of the time! You truly do need to have excellent technical and leadership skills to lead projects successfully. However, there is one area where it does work, and that's in *self-confidence*. The more you act confidently (even if you aren't so at that moment), the more confident you will be. The more confident you are, the more you'll act confidently, and so on in a positive upward spiral.

    Another benefit of being self-confident is that you will be more comfortable taking risks. The more you choose, the more confident you'll be about taking the next one, and so on.

    How can you fake being confident? Start with how you stand and deliver when you're talking to other people. Smiling shows confidence, as does looking people in the eyes and standing up strong and tall. Fidgeting, looking away, mumbling, talking fast, and facing away from the person you're talking to all signal a lack of confidence.

    Also, dress well, especially when you're networking or speaking in front of an audience. Make sure everything fits and is clean with nothing that needs mending. Fiddling with loose buttons or threads will not make you appear confident.

    You can use power poses to help psych yourself up (just not in front of other people, as noted in the section about being assertive above.) Again, stand straight but not rigid; plant your feet wider than shoulder-width apart; and stand with your hands on your hips in a Superman pose for a few minutes.

- **Work on self-confidence**

    There are other ways to build up your confidence besides faking it. When you know, you'll be facing something difficult—like an interview or an annual review with your supervisor—prepare ahead of time and do your homework.

When you're dealing with people you don't know, look them up beforehand on LinkedIn, as well as the company. Gather any intelligence you can on other social media sites and decide how you can be of service to them. What problems do they face? Be an expert on them when you eventually meet them.

Employers will ask plenty of general questions during interviews, such as "Where do you think you'll be five years from now?" or "Give me an example of a problem that you solved in the past." Have answers to these questions ready when you walk through the door.

Otherwise, you may need to prepare some facts for your boss, such as all the money you've saved the company with your productivity system or testimonials from clients who are pleased with your work. If you know you made mistakes, and your boss will bring them up, prepare what you'll say so you can respond calmly and logically. Show how you learned from that error.

For any situation, create and maintain a list of your accomplishments. Everything counts, even the small ones. Sometimes, the small wins are what will keep you going until you can achieve a bigger result. Before you go into a situation that will likely make you tense or feel less than confident, study your list. Remind yourself of what you have done rather than focusing on what you haven't.

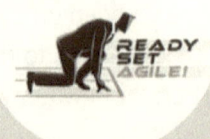

Key Takeaways

Successful project managers are leaders and develop leadership, interpersonal, and communication skills.

- There are specific capabilities that strong leaders have, such as a bias toward action and being independent decision makers who ask for others' opinions when appropriate.
- Modern leaders develop their emotional intelligence, so they can inspire and motivate their team.
- As a project manager, you're responsible for setting the vision for everyone and coaching your team to work their best to achieve the goal.
- Interpersonal capabilities are crucial for PMs, and those who feel lacking in some areas can work on them to improve.

In the next chapter, you will learn how to deal with politics and problems.

---

[1] https://www.russellreynolds.com/insights/thought-leadership/making-it-to-the-top-nine-attributes-that-differentiate-ceos
[2] https://en.wikipedia.org/wiki/Trust,_but_verify
[3] https://www.psychologytoday.com/us/basics/emotional-intelligence
[4] https://www.entrepreneur.com/article/239831

CHAPTER 2

GOT A PROBLEM?

CRITICAL skills required for leaders include solving problems. You know Murphy's Law: if something can go wrong, it will! This is especially true for projects because they are complex in many aspects. Although your team members should have the knowledge and authority to deal with smaller issues that pop up from time to time, you're responsible for handling the big, tough ones. Not only do you need to solve them, but you must do so quickly and effectively, so the team can get back to focusing on finishing their tasks as soon as possible.

Problems in Projects

Sometimes, you'll be dealing with relatively small and insignificant problems, though you should mostly leave them to your team.

However, you should pay attention to the bigger ones that would be beyond your team's capabilities or require your bird's-eye view to solve. On the other hand, sometimes you need to kick away the small pebbles, just so your team can have a smooth surface to travel on.

Here are some of the major challenges that project teams may face.

- **Insufficient resources**

    No one wants to throw away good money when a problem arises. But sometimes the answer really *is* to provide more money, people, or time to take care of it.

    The way to preempt this type of problem is to plan the resource allocation better. Know upfront how much you need to complete the project successfully. If it will take two teams of six people each, then budget for twelve people—not just ten or eleven to make the budget "look" better. During planning, overestimate the required resources to account for any unforeseen issues.

    If it's a project you haven't led before or tasks you're not familiar with, ask. The client themselves may have completed a similar project, or someone else on your team has. Get their input and review case studies. Like the Boy Scouts, be prepared.

- **Poor planning**

    This problem falls squarely on your shoulders as the project manager. You are ultimately responsible for the planning and execution of the project. If you don't plan correctly, even a flawless execution will not allow you to reach your goal.

    Know how to prioritize, break down the work into manageable and measurable tasks, and estimate the time and resources involved.

Again, if you haven't worked with a project like that before, ask for help and find experts who know how to steer you in the right direction.

- **Gap in leadership**

    Lack of leadership will hurt you at the client level, and sometimes it's a result of a gap in your own skills. If the project sponsor or key manager with the client isn't an effective leader, you may find it more challenging to secure a win.

    By the same token, if you need to work on your leadership skills, get going on those *yesterday*! You probably won't be natural in many aspects, but practice and improve. Remember that you don't just have to exercise these abilities at work—you can also find ways to develop them at home or school. We will cover many essential leadership skills within this book.

- **Personnel issues**

    When people work together, there will be conflicts. Some left unresolved will almost certainly torpedo your chances of success. We'll discuss managing conflict in the next chapter. In the meantime, just make sure to encourage members to work together and with the stakeholders.

    You can set a good example by using your listening and communication skills to deal healthily with people who disagree with your tactics, are unmotivated, or have other issues. Model these capabilities for all others involved in the project.

- **Vague requirements**

    It's tough to deliver a project successfully when you don't know what success means, or when they change abruptly and halfway through the process. Make the requirements clear and measurable from the start and document them. If the client continues to provide vague answers, you need to repeat the parameters until you get the ones you can use.

If someone requests a change, make sure you have written into the plan that you must approve it before moving forward. That way, you can prevent the project from drifting and scope creep.

- **Stakeholder issues**

    Sometimes, the stakeholders aren't sure or clear about what they want, or you may have missed a critical constituency that shows up when you're almost finished. In response, the stakeholders may complain that they can't use the result. They may want to increase the scope without providing additional resources or be disinterested in the project's success and not helpful when you need their input.

    Identifying everyone involved and letting them know what's in it for them will be crucial to your success. Communicating effectively with all stakeholders and getting them involved is critical, so you'll need strong stakeholder management skills as a PM.

There are also smaller issues that you'll need to deal with along the way. Most projects have several moving parts, each with its own deadline. For example, the project may involve two devices, and you're not sure how they connect. You would develop a prototype for the connecting bit and test it. Until you've resolved that issue, you will be unable to move forward.

Steps for Solving Problems

There's a basic 5-step framework for doing so. As always, the devil is in the details.

1. Characterize the problem accurately

Before you can solve the problem, you need to define it precisely. If you end up trying to solve the symptoms rather than the disease, you'll take longer because whatever fix you decide on won't take care of the issue.

Suppose the client complains about one of your team members. Is the problem that the team member is a poor worker, or that their communication skills need some work? Were the client's expectations set too high? You can see that the solutions you come up with will differ, depending on how you diagnose the problem.

2. Determine the root cause

There will be times when the cause will be apparent, though you should still perform some analysis to ensure that you're not missing or omitting anything. In other cases, you'll need to dig more. The first cause that you stumble upon may not be the true reason, so you need to work to find the root and ensure that the problem doesn't recur in the future.

- **Fishbone diagram**

    This type of diagram (also called the *cause and effect* or *Ishikawa* diagram) helps teams figure out the main cause of a problem. The problem is stated and a line drawn horizontally next to it, which forms the "spine" of the fish.

    Next, the team determines the main categories of the potential causes of the problem. Each category is drawn on a diagonal line to the spine with some above and some below. They typically include Method, Machines, People, Environment, Materials, and Measurement (ASQ, n.d.)[5]

    Now the team can brainstorm possible causes of the problem for each category.

- *Flowchart*

    This may be particularly helpful when your problem relates to a specific process or workflow. Use or create a flowchart of how the work proceeds along its path, then identify the choke points where the process gets held up. This type of visual aid is great for linear thinkers.

- *Five Whys*

    A popular root cause analysis framework is the Five Whys (Wikipedia, 2020).[6] You would ask why the problem occurred, and when you get an answer, ask why the answer happened, and continue going deeper. You may only need to ask why three times, or you may need to ask more than five times. However, if you keep asking, you'll eventually get to the root.

    Suppose you decided that the client's complaint referred to the team worker's communication skills. Why did they send an email that offended the client? Because they were trying to lighten the mood and missed the mark. Why were they trying to lighten the mood? They were worried that the client would be upset because the deliverable would be delayed a week. Why is the deliverable being delayed a week? Because the critical material was not ordered on time. Why wasn't the order made on time? Because no one knew the material would be needed upfront. Why did no one know? Because the project was new to everyone on the team.

    And there you have it. The root cause of the client's complaint was essentially poor planning upfront!

You want to check that the cause is likely to be the culprit. Does it explain all the phenomena you've seen related to the problem? Depending on what it is, you can probably run a test to confirm that such is the root cause. Take that opportunity when you can, so you don't end up solving the wrong problem and have to go through the process again later.

3. Brainstorm or mind-map solutions

Here's where you and the team would get creative. Make sure the atmosphere for any brainstorming or mind-mapping sessions is open and inclusive. No idea is stupid, though the team may decide later that it's unworkable. Get all the ideas into the open before you start winnowing down.

Finding potential solutions in a group is more valuable than one person doing it alone. For one thing, more minds would generate more ideas. If your team is diverse enough and with different backgrounds, it should be coming up with various ideas.

Brainstorming works best when no one feels ashamed or unworthy. Someone may come up with an idea that isn't quite what the team was looking for, but others could find that it sparks another idea, and that would be how you find creative answers that work.

4. Pick the optimal one

With a functional, creative team, you might well end up with several solutions that work. As the project manager, you should be aware of the project's priorities in terms of timeframe, cost, and quality.

As you could see in my previous book, *Being an Effective Project Manager*, you can pick two of the three: fast, cheap, or good. Which solution maximizes the priority? If there's more than one, which of them optimizes for your second priority?

5. Execute

Going through the problem-solving process is great, but you cannot actually solve it until you implement the answer you found in step 4. Do so decisively and move on. If you're waffling about implementing the solution, you may need to go back to the previous step and confirm that you've chosen the right solution.

Complex Projects

The five-step model above is a pretty simple framework. Often, when you're working on a project, there will be added complexities or other considerations to take into account.

- **The interrelatedness of systems and machines**

    In the old days, it might have been a simple matter to isolate the cause of a malfunction and repair it. Machine #4 had grit in the gears, so it was fixed quickly with cleaning and some lubricant.

    Today, however, most systems are interrelated. Machines are often guided by software, and when something breaks down, you may need to call in the IT department instead of a mechanic.

    Such makes problem solving more complicated. You need to consider all systems involved with a specific machine as potential causes, and isolating the variables can be tricky.

- **No quick fixes for long-term problems**

    The bias toward action and urgency that many people feel when an issue arises may lead to poor problem solving. You could create a Band-Aid for the problem, but how long will it last? Will you be merely delaying a long-term fix in favor of repeating a short-term one? At what point does that become more costly than taking a bit longer to implement a repair that will solve the issue over the long run?

    Eliminating possible causes makes it easier to conduct the root-cause analysis and will prevent you from trying to solve the wrong problem. In fact, according to one PMI conference paper, the first objective should not be to solve the problem but to avoid doing something stupid (Morfin, 2000).[7]

- **Who needs to be involved**

    Teams that believe they're under pressure to solve the problem quickly might try to answer the problem themselves, assuming that it will be faster. However, it may not be the optimal answer.

    Consider the stakeholders involved. If they object to the solution that your team devises, you'll have lost a lot of time. In some cases, stakeholders need to be involved in one or more intermediate steps of the process: data gathering, brainstorming, and choosing the optimal solution.

    This is particularly true if you're having difficulty choosing between two strong options—the stakeholders can help you by expressing their priorities. Don't hinder your problem-solving process by ignoring valuable input from others.

- **Specify the problem**

    Be precise about the problem. For example, "Productivity is too low" is vague, and your team members may object strenuously to that kind of summary of the problem. "The widget production is a week behind schedule" is a specific way to state what's happening and avoid presupposing blame.

    A great way to gather information is to ask "is/is not" questions, allowing you to eliminate potential causes more quickly. For example, where is the issue happening, and where is the issue *not* happening? If widget production on Assembly Line A is a week behind but right on time on Line B, you can focus on Line A to identify the cause.

    When does it happen and when does it *not* happen? Widget production falls behind when Machine 1 is down, but not when Machine 2 is down.

    Give it some parameters. How big is the problem? How big could it be?

- **Data overload**

    We've talked about the necessity of making decisions based on imperfect data. In the modern world, everyone is drowning in data. This makes solutions more difficult because first you have to figure out what is related and relevant to the problem. Most information will probably be nothing more than a *distraction*.

    Relevant information will be precise about the problem and support the goal directly. It's must-have information, whereas much of what you'll see is only nice to have.

- **Avoid analysis paralysis**

    Directly related to data overload, many modern teams find it all too easy to lapse into spending too long on the analysis. Throw out data that isn't relevant and only useful in distracting from the main problem. Sticking with your list of data-gathering questions will help you and the team to avoid collecting unnecessary information. Avoid delaying the last few steps of the process when you don't have to.

    Spending too much time in the analysis is a form of procrastination. If you and the team are not confident in your problem-solving abilities, this may prevent you from taking the steps necessary to implement a solution.

Politics

Whenever you have people, you'll have politics. Don't pretend that the issue doesn't exist, ignore it, or work around it as if it will just go away. To complete the project successfully, you'll need to ensure that interpersonal issues are resolved.

Identifying likely allies and skeptics upfront will help you tailor the message specifically to them. The more influential people you have on your side, the better. You can enlist their help in dealing with those who are unsure of or actively opposing the project. Finding influencers isn't always easy because you cannot use titles as proxies. There may be someone who is listened to by many in the organization while having little to no executive authority. Determining ahead of time who is ready and willing to champion you and the project will get you closer to success.

What distractions pull time and attention away from your project or might affect your champions? Understanding all active forces in the organization is helpful as well. Be aware of other projects that are happening concurrently.

Also, try to discover whether the company had embarked on similar change efforts before you got there. What were the results? If a previous project failed, you must understand the factors and that some skepticism about the projects' wisdom has probably infected much of the staff.

Your team's performance is important too. When they're doing well, make sure you communicate that, especially to the project sponsor and any other project champions you identified. When they're not, it's up to you to figure out how to get them back on track. Do they need more resources? Coaching? Communication with stakeholders is similarly crucial. You can transmit your excitement and keep them interested and engaged in its success.

In addition to politics, when there are people, there will be conflict. We'll discuss how to handle it healthily in the next chapter. In fact, healthy conflict can drive better solutions for problems because you're listening to different viewpoints.

You and your team can use politics positively to help you influence others. Seen another way, you're building and developing a network that can help you and your team succeed.

- **Create a good impression**

    Make sure the important people find you knowledgeable and approachable. They may be senior management or influencers within the department. You don't have to bend over backward, but it would be a good idea to pay them special attention.

- **Nurture mentor opportunities**

    A fundamental characteristic in most people is the desire to help others. People to whom you go for counsel feel important and worthy when you ask them for their advice and feedback. They can become strong allies for your cause as well.

- **Be in the right place at the right time**

    Position yourself to take advantage of opportunities when they come your way.

- **Be strategic in your appointments**

    Make sure that you're taking the time to visit senior executives, management, stakeholders, and influencers. Let them know about you and your team's accomplishments and progress.

    Communicate when there's a way that you can help them personally. They may or may not take you up on it, but the mere offer is powerful. Managers and leaders notice proactive people and prefer them.

- **Build your "favor bank"**

    Favors are usually thought of as reciprocal: you scratch my back; I'll scratch yours. By doing things for others, even or especially when they don't benefit you directly, you're building up favors. When you need one, you'll have plenty of people to ask.

Politics can also be used negatively. Avoid the following because you'll be seen as less of a leader when engaging in these unconstructive behaviors. Remember that trust is built over a long time, but it can be lost very quickly. If you want a good reputation, then avoid the following in all situations.

- **Feinting**

    If you pretend to be interested in one alternative but are using the pretense to take another maneuver, you're destroying the trust that people may otherwise have had in you. A similar situation would be allowing someone to believe that the project is in one condition when, in reality, it's another.

- **Deceiving**

    You already know that honesty—including emotional honesty—is a crucial concept for any leader. Lying for any reason shows a fake facade.

- **Entrapping**

    Manipulating anyone into a bad position where they could lose face, a promotion, or even a job is something that no good project manager would ever stoop to doing. Whether you like or dislike someone is irrelevant.

    It may seem in the short term that getting rid of someone who opposes the project will increase its chances of success. However, that's an illusion. There may be more than one person who's skeptical of the project, so removing one obstacle won't solve the problem.

- **Backbiting**

    Making up negative information or curating a story to show someone in a bad light is another maneuver doomed to fail, and it will hurt your reputation. Good leaders are guided by their values; they don't allow short-term calculations to ruin their long-term opportunities for success.

Does it seem like politics and leadership are two completely separate concepts or ends of a spectrum? When used appropriately, politics can be an essential part of leadership. No one can do everything alone, including the completion of a successful project. As a PM, you'll need to rely on others to support you and help you carry the message. Politics—or using your powers of influence and persuasion—is nothing more than a way to build up your group of allies.

It will assist you in keeping your project on track, and you can then avoid potential political landmines. Knowing where they all are at the beginning is helpful in this regard. Understanding how to use your influence constructively will also help you shield your team from negative political consequences, so everyone can stay focused.

Key Takeaways

Problems and politics occur on every project, and a successful project manager acknowledges them to resolve issues effectively.

- A few common problems tend to crop up in projects, including stakeholder and personnel issues, vague requirements, and insufficient planning.

- A five-step model in solving problems is useful as a framework for any issue that arises.

- Particular attention must be paid to finding the root cause of the problem to ensure that your solution will completely fix the issue, and you won't have to revisit it later.

- Politics can be used either constructively or destructively. When you use your powers of influence for good, you increase your chances of success significantly.

In the next chapter, you will learn how to manage and appreciate conflict.

---

[5] https://asq.org/quality-resources/fishbone
[6] https://en.wikipedia.org/wiki/Five_whys
[7] https://www.pmi.org/learning/library/appraisal-situation-problem-solving-projects-492

CHAPTER 3

FIGHT!
LEARN TO LOVE
THE CONFLICT
YOU'RE IN

CONFLICT is a feature—not a bug when done right. It means that you have a diverse group of people with different backgrounds and opinions. A hive mind, where everyone thinks alike and has essentially the same experience, doesn't have conflict. It also does not produce innovative or optimal solutions to the problems it faces. Leadership requires you to encourage the expression of healthy conflict and eliminate or reduce destructive conflict.

Inevitable Conflict

Just as problems and politics always arise when you have more than one person in a room, so too does disagreement. Ignoring the discord doesn't mean it's not there. In fact, it may even be more dangerous if it's simmering beneath the surface rather than out in the open. Unresolved conflict doesn't go away, and it often boils over just when things are at their worst.

Particularly with more diverse teams, the human brain works against collaboration because it has a tendency to divide the world into *Us vs. Them*, and anyone who isn't clearly *Us* must, by definition, be *Them*. The brain has two systems that balance trusting others and preparing for an attack.

Our old friend, the *amygdala*—where the fight-or-flight reaction resides—is key in distrusting something that might be harmful, like a predator. Remember that on the savannah, humans were in danger of being killed by other animals, unlike in the modern world. We still have that instinct, as we've discussed in my book *Being an Effective Project Manager*.

On the other hand, we also have the mesolimbic system that provides rewards and pleasure for things that will help the brain flourish and survive. This system releases "happy" neurochemicals, such as dopamine and oxytocin, known to promote bonding between people. Our brains are tilted a bit more toward distrusting new people than bonding, yet that can be overcome with good leadership (Henderson, 2018).[8]

Another cause of conflicts between people has ironically increased with the adoption of agile methodology and its reliance on self-organizing teams. Disagreements escalate when people's roles become ambiguous or poorly defined (Villax et al., 2010).[9]

When there's a clear hierarchy and everyone knows exactly what they're doing, there's little opportunity for miscommunication about the order of things. However, when most of the team is cross-functional, and they must decide among themselves who is responsible for which tasks, disputes often arise. Everyone's sense of fairness must be satisfied, and all must be perceived to be carrying the load equally.

It's not helpful for the team to disagree and argue with each other constantly. After all, the work needs to get done. There are a handful of leadership skills that the project manager can use to avoid unnecessary conflict, which is the kind that serves no purpose other than to be a distraction.

- **Team building**

    Sometimes, people just don't understand each other. When they don't spend much time together, they're less likely to give each other the benefit of the doubt. They'll only collaborate with those they trust.

    Diverse teams demonstrate the importance of having members spend time together. When they don't know each other, it will be more likely that the *Us vs. Them* dichotomy is activated. However, as they spend time together, discover how much they're actually alike, and find some common ground, the balance starts to tilt the other way toward the social pleasure system.

    The key to team building is that the team must spend time together and away from the pressures of the project and learn how their different styles and ideas complement each other. You'll uncover more details about team building later in the book.

- **Negotiation**

    Project managers must be skilled at finding win-win solutions wherever possible. Being able to identify a solution that would allow all parties to feel they got something they wanted out of the deal helps build a foundation for more collaboration and clear away potential resentment.

    When the PM finds solutions upfront, it becomes easier for the team and stakeholders to work together. We will discuss more about successful negotiation in a later chapter.

- **Problem solving**

    As you know from the previous chapter, spotting issues when they arise is key to managing a situation. If there are any apparent conflicts at the onset of the project, the PM can address and resolve them before they disrupt the work.

On the other hand, there will be times when open conflict is necessary and helpful. Managed properly, it can provide some space for those with differing viewpoints to air and explain their views while helping the team arrive at an optimal solution.

Styles of Conflict Management

Most people naturally fall into one of five categories when faced with conflict (Planisware, 2020).[10] However, that doesn't mean you can't adopt other styles when necessary. You do need to understand your own type and its advantages and disadvantages. If destructive aspects of the situation get in the way of resolving conflicts, you may apply any of the following styles to fix the issue.

1. The Competitor

This type often believes there is a finite amount of resources; therefore, if someone gets more than them, they must, by definition, receive less. They are assertive and may exert power at the expense of others.

Advantages: useful when a decision is urgent and needs to be made quickly.

Disadvantages: may cause resentment among others and forego the opportunity to find a win-win that benefits all sides.

2. The Avoider

As you can probably guess, this person does not want to get involved in the conflict and will evade it, accept decisions made by default, and delegate decisions that might hurt someone's feelings.

Advantages: when the stakes are low and the context trivial, ignoring the conflict can help the team move on.

Disadvantages: when the stakes are high and nontrivial, pretending conflict doesn't exist can result in a bigger issue down the road.

3. The Accommodator

They're cooperative and will give up their own concerns to satisfy others.

Advantages: when cooperation is needed, this attitude is constructive.

Disadvantages: the Accommodator may end up resenting others, and their concerns may be missing when looking for an optimal solution.

4. The Collaborator

People of this type try to find win-win solutions. They don't back down from their concerns, but they also consider others' needs with respect. They are assertive and inclusive.

Advantages: most likely to resolve conflicts to the satisfaction of all involved.

Disadvantages: none.

5. The Compromiser

As you would expect, this type expects everyone to give up a little something to reach a solution. They give up less than the Accommodator but more than the Competitor.

Advantages: useful when time is tight and no one will budge.

Disadvantages: may miss out on opportunities to find a win-win.

Types of Conflict

Over the years and in terms of project management, conflicts have been viewed differently (Villax et al., 2010).[11] First, the *traditional* view was that it was dangerous and should be avoided, which would have been the manager's viewpoint. Next, the *behavioral* concept suggested that, although conflict should be avoided when possible, it is natural and expected. Although conflict in itself is not healthy, it can be resolved in a way that does not harm.

Finally, the *interactionist* viewpoint believes that conflict should be encouraged up to a certain point because it helps increase performance. Airing different views increases innovation and improvement. It drives the organization to find solutions and, when handled well, improves the firm's creative energy.

However, not all types of conflict are healthy and resolved easily to the satisfaction of all. Some should be avoided or eliminated as best the PM can while allowing healthy conflicts generate benefits. Let's look at the different types of conflicts.

- **Interpersonal**

    This type can easily lead to unhealthy conflict. It can be intense and the damage long-lasting, with emotions running high. Chances of project success with people-focused conflict diminish.

    Fostering a spirit of team harmony and encouraging team building are essential for PMs to avoid interpersonal conflict. Otherwise, the team's effectiveness would be decreased, and the project manager must spend too much time dealing with the fallout.

- **Interface**

    When the team clashes with external forces, such as other stakeholder groups, it can also harm their performance. This conflict is also people-focused and typically occurs when different social groups have contrasting attitudes toward the project, especially when the project is large and involves the community.

PMs can decrease this conflict's likelihood by ensuring they identify and reach out to all stakeholders and communicate with them regularly.

- **Global**

    When the project reaches across the world, it's known as global. Culture, language, work style, and other differences are factors behind this people-focused disagreement. National norms, time issues, and inadequate communication all contribute to it.

    When project managers are assigned to such a project, they need to examine the norms and expectations from all different groups represented in the project. Training and experience will help them determine how deep the issues run and how easily they could be resolved. Improving communication is an excellent first step for many of these conflicts.

- **Task-focused**

    Finally, we have reached the type of disagreement that can be advantageous to the organization. When there are no disputes, the team may not realize that inefficiencies exist or know where they're located. Non-routine and complicated tasks especially benefit from differing opinions, so the team can scrutinize the issue more closely and take time to deliberate.

    However, even task-focused conflict—based on work and not on people—can still decrease the team's performance when the right ingredients are missing. For it to resolve in victory, there must be high trust among the team members. They should feel comfortable bringing up unpopular opinions. The team must be a safe and open space for all members to discuss their views. Thus, an attitude of collaboration is necessary.

PMs can encourage healthy conflict by allowing the team members to come to a resolution themselves, without interfering or micromanaging. They may also engage in "mining," or bringing sensitive topics to the forefront for the group to consider and discuss.

What happens when conflict isn't allowed to or just doesn't appear? One problem that often leads to a lack of necessary conflict is groupthink, which typically occurs when the team is homogenous and from similar backgrounds and experiences. Their decision-making is faulty because they don't consider alternatives, and they would rather be in harmony than make quality decisions that rest on disagreement.

NASA demonstrated this. Previous success in the space program led to complacency. The teams were cohesive and under pressure to make the right decisions, and they eventually fell into groupthink. Rather than criticizing each other's suggestions, finding alternatives, and asking for expert opinions, they censored themselves and rationalized their issues. Ultimately, groupthink was named as one of the root causes for the Columbia and Challenger failures (Villax, 2010).[12]

Resolving Conflicts

There are five strategies that a project leader and their team can use to work through conflict. Some are more likely to result in success, but unfortunately, not all methods will fit all situations. PMs need to decide which strategy would be best to use, depending on the scenario and circumstances. At some point, you will be the one held accountable for getting the team moving again, and you must take charge of that decision.

In order from most likely to encourage project success to least likely, here are the five techniques.

1. Win-win

This process is most desirable because all parties seek a win and understand that a win for others does not mean a loss for themselves. As a PM, unless you're involved directly in the situation, let the team work it out. It requires high trust levels among those working to find the solution, so everyone can be open and willing to discuss and collaborate.

"Win-win sees life as a cooperative arena, not a competitive one. Win-win is a frame of mind and heart that constantly seeks mutual benefit in all human interactions. Win-win means agreements or solutions are mutually beneficial and satisfying." —Stephen Covey[13]

When using this method, the team wants to find the best solution and not necessarily the one that would avoid hurting feelings or repressing valid viewpoints for the sake of team harmony. If the parties are not coming to a common solution, you should push their attention toward the positive aspects.

However, when you have two parties whose viewpoints are diametrically opposed, you may be unable to reach a win-win solution.

2. Compromise

The next most desirable technique is having all parties give up something to attain a mutually satisfying outcome. No one would get all that they want, but everyone can get at least something.

If the win-win technique doesn't work for one reason or another, the project manager can try to compromise. All parties must come to the table without too much power imbalance. They should be willing to make the necessary trade-offs because they want to find a solution.

3. PM decides

Sometimes as the project manager, you may need to force a solution. When parties cannot come to an agreement, it may be up to you to choose a solution. This can work when you're under deadline pressure and the people involved have drawn lines in the sand and aren't budging. They need to respect your decision and agree to abide by it for this to resolve the situation.

However, some people may feel resentment toward the outcome, and it could easily result in another conflict down the road. It's obviously not a preferred option, so you should only attempt this when neither of the first two methods has a chance of resulting in a favorable outcome.

4. Smoothing over/Facilitating

When the stakes are relatively low, but one side is entrenched in their position, you might consider using this method, which is merely another way of saying *pick your battles wisely*. Although emotions tend to run high in any conflict, some disagreements aren't worth spending much time and energy on. Finding the minimum common ground and moving forward is a decent way to deal with relatively unimportant battles.

As with forcing a decision, smoothing over the conflict won't necessarily resolve it permanently, and it often ends up reappearing in the future.

5. Withdrawal/Ignoring

The least favorable way to handle disagreement is to withdraw from it entirely. It's least effective because nothing gets resolved. You're kicking the can down the road, which usually results in its reappearance. The PM must be aware of whether one or more team members are dealing with apparent conflict before withdrawing from or ignoring it. That typically results in resentment and stress building up over time, and you want to head that off when possible.

In addition to having discussions with team members individually about what they're experiencing, you probably need to encourage more openness among the team. Promote issue raising and emotionally intelligent debate, which means that no one will be shamed for their views or be afraid to discuss them.

Key Takeaways

Although many people consider conflict to be a bad thing, when used healthily and constructively, it can increase the team's chance of success.

- Conflict is a feature, not a bug, so PMs need to deal with it constructively.

- Most people have a preferred way of handling conflict, but it may not be constructive, so they need to learn how to manage it for the team's benefit.

- Some types of conflict are inherently unhealthy—especially those that are focused on people—but a task-focused conflict should be encouraged and promoted in the right atmosphere.

- There are five methods for solving conflicts that project managers should be aware of, and two of them (win-win and compromise) are most likely to result in a constructive resolution of the issue.

In the next chapter, you will learn about building your ideal team.

---

[8] https://www.scientificamerican.com/article/why-our-brains-see-the-world-as-us-versus-them/
[9] https://www.pmi.org/learning/library/understanding-managing-conflict-resolution-strategies-6484
[10] https://www.planisware.com/hub/blog/conflict-management-guide-project-managers
[11] https://www.pmi.org/learning/library/understanding-managing-conflict-resolution-strategies-6484
[12] https://www.pmi.org/learning/library/understanding-managing-conflict-resolution-strategies-6484
[13] The 7 Habits of Highly Effective People by Stephen Covey, New York, NY 2013

THERE IS NO "I" IN TEAM

AS a project leader, you need a reliable team that will collaborate with you to complete your project successfully. You may not always have the opportunity to select and hire your team members. However, you would still be instrumental in creating a team that works well together with the emotional space to address difficult issues and develop creative solutions to problems. The PM needs to manage the team in a way that promotes achievement and build it into a well-functioning unit.

The Importance of Teams

Groups of people working together have always been capable of achieving much larger goals than one person working alone. Hunters brought down large prey by working with each other, and one man didn't build the Great Pyramid of Giza.

In more recent years, as command-and-control leadership has fallen out of favor due to its limits on reacting quickly enough to changes on the ground, team members have taken on more responsibility to organize themselves and distribute the work. As a project manager, if you've ever worked in agile, you would know that this kind of self-organization is key to the success of those teams.

Today's businesses are sophisticated and have many relationships with other firms and organizations. The work is complex and highly detailed, and few people can master all intricacies involved in the project. Having a team of people who can tackle a problem and resolve it is necessary for getting work done and moving on to the next issue.

Globalization and technology put a lot of pressure on companies to adapt quickly and do everything better, faster, and cheaper. The modern world requires teams of people to collaborate to deal with these pressures.

Team Management

When the team is functioning like a well-oiled machine, it can be very productive. Successful project managers reduce tension within the team by addressing it when it occurs. They help everyone build trust with one another and remove any type of interpersonal grit that might otherwise get stuck in the gears and prevent the team from moving forward smoothly. It's critical to recognize that today's teams operate in an atmosphere of complexity and must spend more time with related issues and personnel because projects cannot operate in a vacuum.

In a study conducted on multiple projects within a three-year span, five factors were found to be fundamental for team success

(Thamhain, 2007).[14] Interestingly, they're not what managers often think of as being key to victory on a project, such as salary, the time the team has worked together, or project size and complexity. The critical factors are more about professional esteem and connecting goals to team members.

1. Most important: the work environment

To achieve the desired outcome, the project must provide professional challenges and stimulation to the team members. High performers aren't content to rest on their laurels or hit a career plateau. They also don't do well with routine tasks that don't provide any stimulation.

Doesn't it sound like the same requirements you have to be inspired as a project manager? Of course, there are often administrative and other bureaucratic tasks that you and the team must complete and that you'd prefer someone else to take care of. When you're running lean, however, you would still need to get them done.

These tasks are always mandatory, but make sure your team can spend enough time on interesting and demanding work.

2. Opportunities for recognition and accomplishments

Good team members want to achieve their goals, and recognition is often an essential part of that. The ability to list their accomplishments on a resume is a matter of pride.

Not to mention that it helps them further their careers. Just like you, competent team members aren't content to stagnate at one level or another. They want to explore and challenge themselves, and being able to point back to their achievements can help them find the next project or position that will allow them to progress further.

3. Ability to solve problems

If your team has difficulty making decisions or resolving issues, it's highly unlikely the members will be able to perform at the level you want. The team must not only have the capabilities of problem-solving, but they must also want to do it.

This requires a proactive approach. Occasionally, you could have a knowledgeable and competent team that can solve problems. However, rather than resolving the issues, the team might allow them to sit and fester unless they're explicitly told to address them. It is much better to have members interested in tackling issues—no matter the size—and clearing them up, so they can move on with their work.

4. Project related to organizational objectives

Positive results are easiest to achieve when the project itself aligns with the organization's core business and helps achieve its strategic objectives.

Securing visible management support is key to completing projects successfully, as you know. However, when the project doesn't affect management or can't see what's in it for them, there's no reason for them to support it. In fact, it's more of a nuisance to them than anything else. Senior executives also won't provide the resources you need because it won't align with their objectives and incentives.

Most people want to work on something that matters. What that means may be different for everyone, but the basic idea is that no one wants "make-work," which are tasks created to keep them busy with no real purpose.

Not having a meaningful project will make your life as a PM harder too. You may not have the resources you need, and you'll have a team that doesn't really want to work on the project. You'll feel like you're trying to roll a boulder uphill every day. There's a difference between a challenge and an impossibility, and the impossible is not fun to work on.

5. Team members' skills and expertise match the project requirements

If you're working on an IT project, team members skilled in car manufacturing won't be a lot of help. You will mostly need coders and developers. Besides specialists in specific functional areas, you may need to include professionals experienced within the business, industry, or process.

Projects vary in complexity. Bringing in a team member who has worked only on simple projects in the past could be an issue when you have a complex one. No matter how smart they are, there's a learning curve they would need to go through first.

You may have a project that's complex, and no one has worked on anything similar before, even you. Rather than hiring team members with little experience, prefer those who participated in slightly less complex projects but have worked on more of them.

The study found other team factors contributing to a project win, such as team leadership, trust, and connection among the team members and clear project guidelines and expectations. You may have heard leaders talk about intrinsic and extrinsic motivators. The *intrinsic* ones are internal to each person and include a sense of working with purpose and being proud of accomplishments. *Extrinsic* are the motivators that managers can often provide, such as salary, bonuses, or time off. It's interesting that the most significant factors in successful teams are intrinsic rather than extrinsic.

It also provides some insight into how PMs can manage their teams best. Creating a supportive work environment is crucial to team success, and allowing team members to fulfill their professional dreams is a way for the project manager to support the team. Good communication is also essential, as it helps with stakeholders and builds mutual trust and respect among team members, which will help decrease unhealthy conflict.

As a PM, you will need to work with senior management to ensure the project is clearly aligned with business objectives, and that company-wide processes—such as purchasing and managerial controls—help the team rather than hinder it. You don't have much control over these policies and procedures, so you'll need to use influencing and persuading skills to get the most favorable environment possible for your team.

Team Improvement Techniques

Once you have a supportive work environment in place, there are other techniques that will help you manage the team. You must monitor each team member's performance, provide them with feedback, help resolve conflict as you learned in the last chapter, and determine whether there are changes you can make to improve the team's performance. You'll need a leader's emotional intelligence to provide feedback in a way that the team member can take it in and use it to improve rather than feel shamed for making a mistake.

- **Performance appraisals**

    The organization may have specific guidelines for writing your performance appraisals. This is a task that many project managers dread, but the procedure can be beneficial when applied appropriately. You help them see where they are having difficulty and make suggestions to help overcome it.

If you're happy with the performance, you will enjoy the appraisal process. You do need to let your good performers know that you are satisfied with what they're doing. You may still have a few suggestions for improvement and growth.

Many people find criticism hard to take, and you need to deliver it firmly, but not too harshly. One way to do this is to sandwich the critique. Give them a positive statement, then make your critique and follow up with another positive comment.

The appraisal won't be of much help if you don't mention specific situations and the work approach they can improve. You might set time aside for a brainstorming session to see if they have any ideas as well, then their goals can be determined appropriately.

- **Recognize and reward**

  I know old-school project managers used to say that rewards and recognition weren't necessary and that the satisfaction from a job well done was the only praise anyone would need.

  That's just not true. Even high performers need an occasional pat on the back or mention in a company-wide announcement for their accomplishments.

  This doesn't mean that everyone would get a trophy! However, those who truly do outstanding work or have achieved great things should be recognized for it.

  Remember that it's not just about the people receiving an award; it's about the people who watch them earn it. They may be inspired to reach higher in their own lives or see how high the bar is set for performance.

- **Observing and conversing**

  Step away from the computer. One of the most effective ways to manage people—particularly when they're high achievers—is to look at and speak with them. What are the issues they're having? What do they think is going well?

The more you can connect with your team members, the sooner you'll know if there's an issue. They'll be more willing to share their thoughts with you and the group and be more accountable when they know there's a space that is emotionally safe for them to do so.

- **Using BECC**

Taking the above technique a little further, try BECC: Bond, Empathize, Connect, and Communicate (Wilson, 2020).[15] This technique will help you empower your team. As you bond and connect with them, you'll discover their strengths, which can be leveraged for the good of the team.

When you're clear on their capabilities, and you've communicated with them, so they understand what you want from them, you'll be more comfortable delegating specific tasks. Give them the power and authority to take on problems that they can resolve.

To be a true leader, you need to be thinking more about making your followers and team members successful and less about your own success. Their achievements (or lack thereof) will reflect back on you.

- **Tracking with an issue log**

On a more mundane subject, you can manage the issues that arise on a project by creating a log to make sure nothing gets missed. You might end up assigning them to a team member or two to ensure they're resolved.

Team Building Stages

Successful projects begin with successful teams, and as a PM, you would lead the team-building effort. You may have team members who have worked together before, have a group of complete strangers, or mix the two. For them to collaborate and work well together, they need to know each other and their strengths and weaknesses. Your EQ as a project manager will give them some psychological space to come together as a team in an atmosphere of trust and respect.

In 1965, psychologist Bruce Tuckman developed the four-stage model for group development, adding on the fifth phase in 1977 (Toggl, n.d.)[16] They would run from the very beginning—when the team first meets—to the end of the project.

1. Forming

When you have a group of people who don't know each other, they can't even be considered a team at that point; it'd be more like a first date or orientation at a new job.

Everyone wants to make a good impression, meaning that they'll all be pleasant and polite to each other. They're excited about the new project and working with new people.

The project leader would use this time to set ground rules, talk about the overall vision, expected timeframe, and individual roles at a basic level. It's not usually a very productive time.

2. Storming

Now the reality of the project has hit everyone. What seemed challenging now may look nearly impossible to the team members, and the initial excitement has gone. It's also the time in many relationships when the quirks that you accepted when you didn't know the person have become incredibly annoying. Personality clashes often arise and team members may question other members or even the guidance of the project manager.

Here's where all your conflict management skills as a PM will come into play. Ensure that conflicts are resolved and not ignored to the best of your ability to avoid bigger issues later.

As you learned in the last chapter, disagreement is natural, and some of it is healthy. Allow the healthy ones to play out, empowering the team to handle them among themselves, and address the unhealthy ones that typically involve interpersonal relationships.

3. Norming

Once conflicts have been acknowledged and addressed, the team can settle down into a more cohesive unit. They may learn to appreciate each others' strengths, and they're starting to collaborate.

You might still see some issues with storming, as it's not always a smooth transition between the two stages, but the conflicts might be easier to deal with once there has been some cooperation.

4. Performing

If the team makes it this far, you will likely get a win on this project. Here they are collaborating, cooperating, and leveraging each other's strengths to be more productive.

They're confident and motivated to work toward the common goal. As a PM, you can feel comfortable delegating more work to them, knowing they're ready and willing to do it. They're eager to reach the destination and optimistic about their prospects.

This is the desired stage—one that many teams never achieve. Most accountability for team success or failure rests on you. If you're not clear on goals or roles and responsibilities in the forming stage, the team will struggle to move through the storming phase. Similarly, if you don't handle the conflict well, the team may be unable to work as a cohesive unit in the norming stage of the process.

5. Adjourning/mourning

At the conclusion of the project, the team would disband. They may actually go through a mourning phase once they're finished with the project, or they may have enjoyed working with the other members and become sad about moving on to something else.

How to Build Your Performing Team

Now that you understand the phases of team development and skills you might need at each stage, you can think about how to develop a successful project team. What are the critical factors in building a team that would help you achieve the fourth stage of development: performing?

- **Choose the right people**

    If you have hiring authority, pick a solid group of people with diverse backgrounds. You will want teammates who challenge each other and avoid falling into groupthink. By the same token, you don't want a group full of divas trying to outshine the others at all costs, either.

    In addition—though, this may go without saying—you need to pick members whose skills and abilities match the project's requirements. You may find some applicants who have a lot of qualifications, at least on paper. But are they qualified for the position you need them to fill?

    Once you've hired them, take some time to discuss with them personally your expectations. Why do you think they're a good fit and their role on the team are some topics to discuss. This will help reduce the anxiety they're likely feeling about embarking on a new project.

- **Set the tone and ground rules**

   If you want the team members to raise difficult topics and feel comfortable owning their own mistakes, you need to demonstrate your high EQ in the beginning. While the team is forming, make sure they understand what you expect from them and what the rules are.

   If there are ambiguities around roles and responsibilities, address them. Now's the time to make goals and roles crystal clear, so no one would be confused or feeling like someone isn't pulling their weight. Bringing clarity while they're forming will help defuse some tension while storming.

- **Communicate a clear vision**

   Likewise, everyone should know exactly what the overall goal is and what they are expected to achieve. You want every person on the team to achieve a win. All individual goals should add up to the overall project goal.

   Remember—you're the ship's captain. The crew members need to know where they're rowing, so they all can head in the same direction. You're the one with the bird's-eye view.

- **Pick small wins**

   If there's an opportunity to celebrate achievements early on, do it. This would be another way to defuse some conflicts in the storming stage. It keeps people motivated when the project hits what appears impossible after the forming phase has ended.

Plan for these small goals early on and make them ones that you believe can be achieved. Reaching them encourages the team going forward and gives them a sense of pride in their work.

- **Be transparent**

    You already know how important communication is to project success. Your team members should be the first to hear any news, after you. Keep them up to date on what's happening with the larger client organization (where it's relevant) and issues that you hear about from the stakeholders.

    The spirit of collaboration that you've fostered should provide an open space for team members to share rather than hoard information. The more clarity you can have with them, the less pressured they are to hold back or release information selectively.

- **Provide feedback after meetings**

    We discussed performance appraisals in a previous section, but more targeted feedback can assist the team as well. There's a place for one-on-ones, but make sure you make space for group feedback as well. Remember the compliment sandwich when you have critiques, so the team won't feel ashamed for making errors.

- **Provide scheduled team-building time**

    You'll be working with the team a lot during the forming phase, both as a whole and with individual team members one-on-one. Even after they've settled into the norming stage, continue to set aside time for team building.

    Small business owners are usually encouraged to set aside time to work *on* their business, not just *in* it. In other words, it is not only about fulfilling customer orders or providing the service, but also about planning and reviewing. Similarly, all should work *on* the team and not just *in* the project.

As noted earlier, you don't have to go off-site, though the occasional evening out or fun activity isn't a bad idea, particularly when morale is flagging. Some of this time could be devoted to short meetings where the team would reflect on what's gone well and what hasn't, then brainstorm ideas for improvement.

How to Break Barriers

There are common barriers that get in the way of effective team building. Fortunately, that means there are also different ways of reducing or even eliminating them as well.

1. Varying viewpoints and judgments of team members

You followed the guidelines on hiring a diverse team, and now interpersonal relationships are threatening the team's success.

- Try to uncover these issues early in the forming stage to address them quickly.

- Give them a very clear station WII-FM (What's In It For Them), so they understand how they will benefit personally from the project.

- Explain how their roles, responsibilities, and interests meld with the overall goal.

2. Ambiguity in roles

This may be less of an issue in waterfall project management, where you would usually be the one responsible for assigning who does what. However, with self-organizing teams, this is sometimes more difficult.

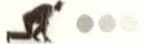

- When you sit down with them individually, understand where they believe themselves to fit within the group.
- Create a work breakdown structure (WBS), so the tasks and associated responsibilities are clear, then assign people as necessary.
- Monitor potential role conflicts throughout the project.

3. Lack of clarity on goals

This burden is on you to a large extent. If you didn't get clarity with the client on what they wanted, you should have continued asking questions until you got it. If you're clear on what they are, but your team members aren't, what you have here is a failure to communicate.

- Keep asking your client/sponsor for more details and reasons.
- Inform your team members and let them ask questions.

4. Changing environments

To some extent, circumstances change over which you have no control. However, there may be other dynamics—such as a desire by the client to squeeze out a little more from the deliverable—that you can resolve as an effective PM.

- Ensure critical stakeholders clarify the overall direction and get the team's buy-in.
- Communicate the dangers of unwarranted changes to the client and their senior management, which will help stabilize the environment.
- Develop your contingency plans.

5. Leadership competition

Similar to role ambiguity, this may be less apparent in traditional project management. Otherwise, in this case, you may not be performing up to the expectations of your team.

- Senior management needs to demonstrate their support of the team lead.
- As a PM, understand what the team expects from you and adjust accordingly. Having clear roles, as noted above, will also help.

6. Lack of structure and definition on the team

Not only does senior management need to be educated and "sold" on the project team, but so does the team itself.

- Senior management and the client must demonstrate their visible support in emails, newsletters, videos, among other forms of social communication.
- Hold regular team meetings.

7. Lack of commitment by team members

As soon as this issue arises, it needs to be addressed. There are a variety of reasons why a member of the team may hold negative views on the project or team itself. The issue is often insecurity, but it could also be a relationship conflict or because the project doesn't satisfy them professionally.

- If they're insecure, try to figure out why and help them allay their fears.
- With a relationship conflict, handle it as you learned in the last chapter as soon as you can.
- If they may be better off elsewhere on a different project that aligns more with their interests, consider finding a replacement.

8. Choosing the wrong people

Depending on who has hiring authority, this may or may not be due to your staffing decisions.

- Negotiate assignments to try to leverage each member's strengths.
- Clarify WII-FM, including the potential rewards, purpose of the project, and rules of engagement.
- If it still doesn't work out, consider replacing them.

9. Project leader credibility

To want to follow you, team members must respect your authority and abilities. If they don't see you as credible, you'll need to repair that image of yourself if you want to move to the performing stage.

- Get visible support from senior management.
- Demonstrate your decision-making and problem-solving skills to the team.
- Demonstrate your technical knowledge.

10. Communication issues

You know how important it is. If you're having difficulty or don't think the team is where it needs to be regarding this skill, try the following.

- Hold regular status reviews and use schedules and the reporting system to facilitate transparency.
- Where you can, colocate the team: have everyone in the same room together.
- Establish regular channels and schedules for conversations with clients and senior management. Ensure key agreements and issues are noted in writing.

11. Lack of support from senior executives

If you read my book *Being an Effective Project Manager,* you learned some techniques for ensuring that you have senior management on board visibly with the team and project.

- Invite them to be a part of the project reviews.
- Ensure they understand what you and the team need from them.
- Develop relationships with key members and sell them on the project's importance for them personally; yes, senior management needs to know WII-FM too!

When you have a high-performing team, it truly captures the spirit of the old adage that *"The whole is greater than the sum of its parts."* Teams that collaborate together achieve significant synergies. Make it so helping each other and cooperating are natural for the team and not considered extra work or a burden. They understand that when they function as a unit and not separate people coming together, they can achieve more, both in terms of the project and for their individual development.

Key Takeaways

The team's function is critical to project success, and project managers should encourage members by managing and building the team according to successful principles.

- Effective team management involves PMs with high emotional intelligence to create an environment of openness and trust.

- There are five stages of team development, and many teams, unfortunately, don't reach the crucial fourth phase known as "performing," where they would act effectively and as a well-oiled machine.

- During team development, the project manager must continuously build the team and work through common barriers to performance.

In the next chapter, you will learn how to develop each member, so they can be their best selves on the project and work to their strengths.

---

[14] https://www.pmi.org/learning/library/managing-project-teams-age-complexity-7212
[15] https://www.ntaskmanager.com/blog/effective-team-management/
[16] https://toggl.com/stages-of-team-development/

CHAPTER 5

PUT ME IN, COACH, I'M READY TO PLAY

AS the *leader* of your project team—not just the manager—you are responsible for developing your team members. You know by now that the top-down management style of the last century is no longer in fashion, and even waterfall PMs are directing their teams less and empowering them more.

On an effective team, members handle most daily tasks and responsibilities, solve work problems, and resolve interpersonal conflicts themselves. This frees up the project manager to handle big-picture tasks and deal with higher-level issues. The more you can trust your team to handle tactical work, the more you can focus on the strategic.

However, your team may not be ready to handle these tasks right away or believe they're prepared. Assuming that you have hired mature team members with a strong work ethic, your focus should be on mentoring and encouraging them rather than directing and micromanaging.

What is Coaching?

As mentioned earlier, one measure of success of your leadership is how much the team flourishes under your guidance. The better they do, the more their results will reflect on you and vice versa; if the team performs poorly, most will assume your weak leadership is a primary contributing factor.

Coaching is correcting behaviors to increase the chances of reaching a goal successfully, whether that be personal or business-related. It's positive and constructive in nature. Top athletes use coaches to improve some aspect of their performance in the sport, and they may have more than one coach to work on different skills. Business executives also use coaches to help them be mature in various areas and level up their performance. It's not the same as mentoring, which we'll discuss a little later in the chapter.

In addition to typical project management skills, such as planning and organizing, a good PM must also be a good coach. Though they may jump in whenever they see the team falling behind or not using resources effectively, there are a handful of areas where PMs typically have the opportunity to help team members improve (Woods et al., 2011).[17]

- Strategic thinking
- Interpersonal skills
- Managing conflict
- Leadership
- Communication
- Versatility

What Benefits Can Team Members See from PM Coaching?

When the project manager coaches, in conjunction with team building, the team can achieve powerful results. Team members are more likely to accept additional tasks. Team building allows for coaching to take place in a constructive and positive environment, which would then lead to working *smarter*, not *harder*.

When one team member is underperforming, coaching can help them learn how to contribute more to the team. Those who are already solid performers learn to share their knowledge with the rest of their teammates and help teach them how to be more productive. Just as a Six Sigma Master Black Belt coaches other Black Belts, the PM can help star performers learn to coach their peers. Leveraging all team resources and sharing knowledge so no information is lost if a star performer leaves is a contingency plan that all project managers should make.

Another valuable bonus of coaching is that it empowers the team. Members learn to think independently and solve problems on their own, which would increase the trust and pride they have in their work, in addition to taking some of the burden from the project manager.

When you develop the project plan, you will be identifying the competencies needed for the various tasks in the project. When you're choosing your team members, ensure they are *coachable*. In other words, they need to be willing to be coached. Some people aren't, maybe because they believe they know everything or for some other reason. Avoid hiring those types of people if you can.

It's not a "one-and-done" effort. With one short talk, it's unlikely you'll be able to turn an underperforming member into a star. Recognize that you'll need to spend regular time with them to get the results you want. Just as team building needs to occur throughout the entire project, so do coaching activities.

Also, assess the willingness of your team members. You may need to build more trust with them before they can be vulnerable to working with you. Evaluate whether coaching is really what the person needs. If they're having difficulty managing their conflicts with other team members, that's one thing; however, if they also can't do their work on time and have poor communication and interpersonal skills, they may need more help than you can give them. Consider having a talk with their supervisor or HR, or replacing them.

Coaching Principles

You can work with your people either one-on-one or as a team. It can be formal or informal as well. If it's formal, you'll probably have a structured way to approach it and a feedback process too. You'll generate reports and set goals to be accomplished. The informal process is more of a catch-as-catch-can model, where you would discuss goals and challenges the person or team is currently facing.

You would set the tone for constructive and positive feedback while supporting the team consistently. As they build trust with you, the coaching effort will become much more relaxed. There are many different frameworks out there, complete with catchy acronyms. Your organization may have one that it wants you to follow, or you could read about it. Whichever one you choose, there are some common characteristics for being an effective coach.

- **Active listening**

    It's not about you and your knowledge, which is the foundation of mentoring instead. In the coaching process, the team member should be talking more while you guide them.

- **Socratic method**

    This form of teaching relies on asking questions. You don't want to give your team members the answers; you want them to figure it out for themselves. Their answers may differ from what you might initially think. They also need to be right for them—not for you.

    Help them reach the answers by asking questions designed to get them thinking.

- **Stimulating inspiration**

    Help your team members be creative and inspired. Keep the focus on them and not you.

- **Flexible**

    Because this process is designed to develop team members, the answers and questions may not be the same for everyone. Even if you're using an existing coaching model, make sure you tailor everything to the person or team you're working with at that moment.

- **Humble**

    You may be surprised by the creative and workable solutions your people can come up with during the process! Understanding that you don't know everything is crucial—not just for building trust, but also allowing them to be emotionally open as well.

- **Focus on the process**

    It's natural for action-oriented personalities to want to have the result completed yesterday. However, that won't be the reality, especially when you're coaching. It takes time for new good habits to form, and your underperformer won't transform into a rock star overnight.

Therefore, look at small improvements. Did your conflict-averse team member stand up for themselves in a meeting? That's progress. Did the person who lacks interpersonal skills make a small step toward recognizing another team member for their hard work? Progress. Track the little improvements, and you'll see that they add up over time.

- **Mutually defined outcomes**

    Managers may tell their staff about the outcomes they expect, but coaches don't. Instead, they work with the participant or team to define the ideal result. Both of you need to trust each other for this to work. They must believe that you have their best interests at heart and are committed to the outcome that you'll both be defining.

Types of Coaching

There are several different types of coaching that are often used within the project management process.

1. Knowledge building

This is the easiest type of coaching and results in the team member obtaining the knowledge they need for the specific project or task—for example, training on project management software. It's used best for new staff or when a new technique or tool is introduced.

2. Soft skills acquisition

Many people have gaps in these skills, which include communication, leadership, and relationship building. This can be done either formally or informally, and individually or with the whole team.

Focusing on soft skills works well when there is conflict within the team or individual members are disengaged from the project or culture.

3. Work-life balance

Why should you, as a PM, provide this kind of coaching? You want to avoid burnout in your team members, for one thing. Don't worry—you won't be a therapist or counselor, but you'll discuss activities such as stress management and self-confidence.

It requires a higher level of and mutual trust between you and the team member than knowledge or skill building. Use it when you have a team member who is dealing with a life issue or seems so stressed out that their work is being affected.

4. Performance

Here's where you would assist your team members with achieving a project goal or objective. It differs from knowledge building because you would have a particular result that you want to achieve rather than general knowledge. An example of performance coaching is working with a team member in conducting successful stakeholder analysis interviews.

5. Stretch/developmental

This is the toughest and most time-consuming way to coach someone, and it requires dedication from both parties. It helps them develop personally, so they can take on more rewarding and challenging projects.

Once you've selected which type of coaching will be most appropriate, you can move through the phases of coaching with them. Bear in mind that since this kind of work often requires multiple sessions to obtain results, you could end up going through the same phases more than once or from one stage back to a previous one to ensure that your coaching sticks.

Coaching Procedures

Some of your team members may need direction. For them, you may need to provide answers or specific instructions for certain tasks. Others may respond better to supportive coaching, where you would spend more time on facilitating new behaviors or building self-confidence. Whether you direct or support in your coaching, you will depend on the person you're coaching and what they need to address.

1. Observe

As a project manager, you should be taking the opportunity to watch your entire team in action. Specifically, you may find someone who isn't keeping up or not displaying the same skills as their peers.

2. Identify gaps

What type of coaching does the person need? They may lack the knowledge, skills, or even self-confidence to perform well. As you determine what they need, you can then identify the kind of coaching they need.

3. Validate

Verify what you've observed with managers and supervisors. You may or may not need to ask some open-ended questions, because their manager could demonstrate that they are also concerned about the team member's gap.

4. Engage

After you've confirmed the person does require particular coaching, invite them to join you. Remember that, although they may have a need, they may not be willing yet to engage in a coaching relationship with you. Clarify for them what your expectations are for the process and how it will work.

5. Collaborate

Once they're OK with engaging with you, share your observations and what you believe the gap is. Notice that this stage is called *collaboration*, not direction! Help them arrive at the conclusion they want to address and improve their performance. Together, decide what help will be required and what the actions should be.

6. Agree

Both of you need to concur on the action plan, goals, and outcomes. Your team member must be willing to put in the work, which means that they understand the plan to be fair and reasonable and take personal responsibility for self-development. You need to see that the plan will serve to make the necessary improvements.

7. Give feedback

Be specific in your constructive criticisms or praise, as appropriate. They need to understand exactly what it is that they're doing wrong or right, so they can either fix it or make sure they incorporate it into their work habits.

They need to know they're on the right track, so make sure you *praise* when you see progress. Most people respond much better to praise than criticism, so make sure you take the opportunity when it arises.

8. Monitor

Just as it's easy for the company to lapse on the progress it's made from making changes, so too can people. Follow up periodically to ensure they haven't slipped back into their old ways and have maintained their progress.

Mentoring Your Team Members

Mentoring is an essential skill that leaders need. A mentor is a trusted advisor to their mentee and guides them either formally or informally toward professional growth and development. In contrast to a coaching relationship, mentoring is about you as a project manager and the specific skills and knowledge you would share with the person you mentor. It requires a longer time commitment and can last from several months to even years.

Not everyone on your team will necessarily want to be in a mentoring relationship, and some of them may not wish to be in one with you. Don't take it personally—understand those team members may want another perspective. You don't want to force anyone into it because they won't want to do the work.

Some organizations set up formal programs for mentorship. Programs support the business objectives and strategic plan for the firm. They may have criteria for mentors in terms of training, ensuring that time is set aside regularly for both parties to meet, providing an orientation for all employees, and overall support from various levels of management.

Smaller companies—or those that have not yet matured in terms of projects—often don't have formal programs set up, so mentorship would occur informally. It's up to the two involved to figure out how to schedule the time to get together, and it's pretty common for the mentee to initiate these types of relationships.

In that case, the mentee should communicate why they want a mentor (e.g., to help with technical skills or navigate a large company's bureaucracy). They would define the background and skills the mentor should pose, identify possible candidates and contact them to see if they might work with them, and follow up with the person who looks promising.

Note that although mentorship is expected from leaders, including project managers, you can also still be someone else's mentee even as you're serving as a mentor. You have the knowledge and skills to guide someone relatively new to project management, but you may want to level up your own skills by working with a program manager who has more extensive experience.

There are several different ways that a mentor can advise their protege, and these can also be combined, depending on the relationship.

- **Source of information**

    The mentor might suggest good professional organizations to join or books to read and helpful conferences that their mentee can attend.

- **Career guide**

    As a PM, you can recommend credentials that someone in the field should have, the types of projects to take on that can satisfy their career goals, and courses they should take. If you're helping someone who wants to follow in your footsteps, you can provide a wealth of information in that regard.

- **Interpersonal guide**

    Effective project managers understand that politics comes along with the job. Someone may need your help navigating informal networks in your organization, or you might assist them in understanding political influencers and how to leverage them.

- **Intellectual guide**

    Here, you'll be helping someone with some of the more technical skills of project management. They might come to you for advice on a specific task or give them feedback on their work. You can then collaborate with them, perhaps on something like a paper for a project management conference. This type of mentoring can be the most helpful in the project management field (Levin, 2011).[18]

Grow as a Mentor

Being trained as a mentor can be helpful when you want to give back to the profession in that way or if your organization requires it. If you need to obtain the training on your own, look for a program that contains the following elements:

- How to develop and document goals with the mentee.
- How to set short-term and long-term goals, with the short-term ones designed specifically for early wins.
- How to develop appropriate metrics to measure success.
- Using open-ended questions to guide the discussions and keep them on track.
- Further developing the mentor's relationship skills, including critical thinking and active listening.
- Using feedback approaches known to foster trust and confidence.
- Working with different generations and personalities.
- Understanding the mentor's personal style.

According to Levin, there are **five characteristics** that a good mentor needs to develop, so their mentees can be successful.

1. A genuine interest in the mentee

This might be more difficult in organizations where mentoring relationships are assigned. However, if the mentor can't develop an actual interest in their mentee's growth and success, it will be hard for them to find the time necessary to meet and mentor them.

2. Being a role model

In other words, the mentor needs to practice what they preach. They should demonstrate behavior and attitude that the organization determines as keys to success. Good mentors lead by example, in addition to providing feedback and advice.

Anyone whose motto is "Do as I say, not as I do" would be a very poor mentor.

3. Providing assistance

As part of the process, be prepared to offer resources, suggestions, and assistance with problem solving. You could discuss examples or stories of previous projects, how similar issues were handled, and the results from the approach taken. People respond very well to stories, so use them when you can.

4. Giving constructive criticism

If you are afraid to be truthful with someone because it might hurt their feelings, you should probably not offer yourself up as a mentor when asked. You need to be clear about what went wrong or what needs improvement; otherwise, the mentee will be unable to grow.

On the other hand, you don't want to crush their spirit either, so you'll need to communicate your feedback supportively. Show them how they can learn from the problem and improve rather than be upset or hindered by a mistake.

Just as with coaching, praise when you have the chance. Make it specific, so they can understand what can put them on the right track.

5. Assisting with motivation

Encourage your mentee to do what's necessary to grow professionally. You might suggest steps they can take to improve their conflict resolution if you see that to be an issue, which will help them solve problems better. Achieving long-term goals takes time, so help them with the small steps they would need to take along the way.

People and Cultures

You may or may not be used to working with project members from a variety of countries or cultures. As companies have globalized, they often need to have project teams made up of staff from different offices around the world. PMs must be comfortable acknowledging and working with these differences, so the team can work cohesively in the performing stage.

Cultures differ in many ways, not just language; you have to be aware of how others think, conduct nonverbal communication, their values, and their behaviors. For example, it's pretty well known that Eastern cultures tend to prioritize the group over the individual, and in the West, it's usually the other way around. In some cultures, women may look down when the PM speaks to them, which is an indication of respect and not shyness. Otherwise, they may not verbally disagree with you when you're talking, which does not actually mean that they agree with you or understand what you've said.

There are differences between generations as well. Generation X (born roughly between 1961 and 1980) and younger generations are more accustomed to a multicultural workplace and having women in positions of authority. Baby Boomers (born 1946-1960) and older do not necessarily have the same level of understanding.

Typical problems that project managers have with multicultural teams include a lack of understanding of all the present cultures, inability to open communication channels between all team members, and ignoring team members' needs whose cultures they're not familiar with. Also, there are often miscommunications and misconceptions among the team members themselves, which lead to conflict and delay.

As a project manager, you can ask yourself how you can interact with each member of the team effectively. How can you open up communication and help resolve some of the inevitable cultural conflicts?

- **Understand the cultures present in your team**

    The best way for a project manager to handle the diversity on their teams is to educate themselves. Recall that a diverse team brings more creative solutions, as long as the environment is psychologically safe for everyone to speak up.

- **Attend cross-cultural workshops and training**

    Given that so many companies have global locations, more resources are dedicated to teaching people how to thrive and help others thrive in these relationships.

- **Be humble**

    Just because you're used to doing things in a certain way doesn't mean that another culture's method is inferior. Demonstrate your openness to learning new things and encourage the team to do the same.

- **Raise difficult issues when necessary**

    Just as you shouldn't ignore conflict that needs to be aired out, don't ignore the elephant in the room. Maybe the entire team needs to attend cross-cultural training, or you have to be the one to raise the issue, so others can feel comfortable discussing it. Don't sweep these kinds of problems under the rug because they will come back to bite you.

Delegation

When you have a team whose members you trust to do their best and solve problems creatively, you'll discover how easy and freeing delegation can be. It's a well-known productivity hack in other fields, and to be a successful project leader, you must master the art of delegating to others.

It's not something that comes naturally for many people. Especially for high performers, because they're used to doing things themselves when trying to make sure the task reaches its best standards. If you are a great expert in some field and want to do it all by yourself, then you should be a team member rather than a project manager.

It's important to note that even though you may delegate a task to someone else, you're still ultimately responsible for it. If the person you delegate to doesn't get it done or performs poorly, that will reflect badly on you. This is another reason why people tend not to delegate: they don't want someone else doing anything wrong when they could simply do the task themselves in the first place.

Why delegate then? What are the benefits that would outweigh the concerns?

- **You don't have time for everything**

    As you know, numerous tasks, duties, and obligations come with the role of a PM. We've discussed the importance of the project manager remaining strategic and taking charge of the high-level vision and execution of the project. When you focus on that, you'll have less time for more tactical or daily tasks.

    You know that your team doesn't have the same overall view of the project that you do, but instead, it has knowledge and skills for daily tasks. Which would make more sense to you—keeping your focus on the strategic vision or performing tasks that your team members are qualified to do?

- **You don't know everything**

    True leaders are humble and know what they don't know. They understand that they and others will make mistakes, and their ideas aren't always the best ones. That's why they include the team when they're brainstorming solutions for problems.

    Once you accept that others also have good ideas, how would you know that the way you approach a particular task is best? Maybe the person you're considering delegating a specific task to is an expert in that field, productive, or has otherwise uncovered the secrets to getting the job done quickly. Maybe they don't, but you won't really know until you give them the task, which would also free up your time to work on something else.

- **As a leader, you're responsible for the growth of your direct reports**

    No one needs robots on a project management team. The PM and all members need to have good critical thinking and problem-solving capabilities while always working on improvement.

    Delegating tasks to your team members gives them a new challenge they can be proud of once they've completed it and potentially a new tool to add to their toolbox. By letting go of something that you know you can do, you provide someone else the opportunity to stretch themselves.

    This is all really what leading a team is all about. It's not about having people who would come in and do the same job day in and day out, but instead, it's about helping them grow. If you don't delegate, you deny your team a chance to develop professionally.

Delegate Tasks with Three Steps

There are three process steps to delegating a task (Stickney et al., 1983).[19]

1. Assign responsibility

First, you must choose who will take on the task, preferably someone you trust and with whom you have a reasonable expectation that they'll complete the job on time. Make sure it will provide them a growth opportunity too.

Try to distribute the rote tasks and more exciting ones equally among the team.

2. Provide the authority

Give the team member the right to act on your behalf and with whatever permissions or resources they need to do so. If anyone should know that the team member owns a particular task, let them know ahead of time.

Also, ensure they have the necessary budget. Avoid sending a team member out to the office supply store to buy whiteboard markers without giving them money for those supplies.

3. Create accountability

There must be a way for you and any other relevant stakeholders to know when the task has been accomplished.

How Best to Delegate

Right now, you may understand the importance of delegation but still be unsure as to how to go about it. Here are some ways to improve your delegating prowess and become more confident in offloading these tasks.

- **Pick the right tasks**

  There may be some tasks that are more difficult to delegate, or for whatever reason, you truly need to keep them for yourself. Tasks that you can assign easily tend to be finite and discrete with clear timeframes and endpoints.

  Ideally, they would also be tactical rather than strategic in nature, and the team member chosen has some familiarity with the topic, even if they haven't performed it before.

- **Share clarity**

  Not having clear guidelines is a recipe for failure in management. If you can't describe it accurately, don't assign it until you can be precise.

  Explain any key or starting points and make sure the team member understands all relevant deadlines—not just the one specific to the task but also any others that could impact it. Both of you should know when the job is done.

- **Don't micromanage the "how"**

  Once your team member understands the task, let them run with it. What's important is the quality of the end result—not how they got there.

  You can provide templates if you think they'll be helpful, but that doesn't mean the team member must use them if they can complete it on their own.

- **Be available for assistance without being a "helicopter parent"**

  In other words, don't hover. The point of delegation is to free up your time for the more strategic obligations that you may have, and watching them working isn't one of those duties.

On the other hand, your team member may need assistance or have questions for you. You can also check in by asking for a draft if they're working on a document or speech. Don't let them believe they've been left on their own to do your work.

- **Team be praised!**

    Be generous and public with your praise, and make sure you're rewarding both effort and outcomes. Share in meetings and emails that the whole team reads. Hopefully, with all the delegation distributed evenly among team members, there will be frequent opportunities to mention everyone's good work throughout the project.

- **No "backsies"**

    If you've chosen tasks that will stretch your team members, they may struggle with it. If someone tries to give it back to you, try to figure out why they're having a problem. Are they feeling overwhelmed by all their responsibilities or by the challenge you provided? Are they disengaging from the project or just being uncooperative? Avoid taking it back unless doing so will prevent a major disaster.

    If delegation is a challenge for you—as it is for so many people—don't allow yourself to take back that task, even if it means a little more work on your part to help your team member get through it. You'll get better at delegating, and they'll grow too with the challenge you've provided. Stay strong.

Key Takeaways

One of the critical components behind being a good leader is developing the individual team members working on the project *with you*.

- Coaching is a relationship where you would help team members improve project-related skills, which may include conflict management and handling interpersonal relationships.

- Mentoring is how you would help guide an individual toward the right opportunities for their career and personal development.

- Multicultural teams often run into issues due to their diversity, and there are ways the PM can help the team work together, despite their differences.

- Good leaders must delegate to their team members, both to free up time better spent on strategic initiatives for themselves and help the team grow.

In the next chapter, you will learn how to get the best from your resources.

---

[17] https://www.pmi.org/learning/library/project-manager-team-coach-plan-success-6251
[18] https://www.pmi.org/learning/library/mentoring-key-competency-program-project-professionals-6264
[19] https://www.pmi.org/learning/library/delegation-sharing-authority-matrix-organizations-1806

CHAPTER 6

LEVEL UP YOUR BEST

THERE are two essential skills that project managers must have to leverage their resources as best they can: *negotiation* and *facilitation*. As with many of the leadership techniques discussed in this book, these are useful tools to have in your personal life as well.

Want to buy a car? Know how to get a better price. Want a higher salary? Know how to start the conversation and demonstrate your value. Want to tackle a specific project? Know what they want from the project and what you can offer as a tradeoff. Want to have a better relationship with your teenage child? Learn to navigate what they can and can't handle, so they can participate in important decisions.

Negotiation

It's a complex skill, but you won't get far without it. It combines many other leadership characteristics, including emotional and traditional intelligence, strategic and tactical thinking, focus on results, ability to listen actively, and conflict management. You can negotiate the scope with stakeholders, prices with vendors, responsibilities with team members, budget with the controllers, and get the best employees from their managers. You may be called upon to negotiate changes in scope during the project, the release to operations, roles and responsibilities, and the boundaries of authority, among other issues.

Put simply, negotiation is how you would find a mutually agreeable solution for a problem that's shared between people.

At this point I would like to encourage you to download the negotiation checklist, which I created as a bonus to this book. You can find a banner with a link at the beginning of this book. The following sections are summarized on the checklist. It will be practical for you when you need to enter negotiation, whether it is on the project or any area of life and need to remember the most important tips and techniques.

There are generally three styles of negotiating (Englund, 2010).[20]

1. Hard

This is a typical negotiating style for those who believe that resources are limited and only one side can get them, which means if you win, then I lose. It's an aggressive approach where the other side would be the enemy.

The hard negotiator bargains competitively to make sure they win; otherwise, they lose. There is no in-between, nor is there a way for all parties involved to come out on top.

2. Soft

Naturally, the opposite of hard is soft. These negotiators—who often tend to be conflict-avoidant—give up more than they should. They believe that the relationship with the other party is more important than what they might get out of the deal.

Pleasing the other side becomes the goal, which results in an agreement reached easily. However, the soft bargainer loses much more than they gained, and the deal they made becomes more than likely a bad one.

Note that there is still no concept of a win-win here in terms of deal outcomes.

3. Principled

By contrast, the principled one sets aside the personalities and relationships from the problem at hand. Rather than focusing on positions, they look toward interests instead.

What's the difference between interests and positions? If I'm going car shopping, I might take up a *position* that I would only purchase a four-door sedan. However, what I actually want from my new car is a place to put my bicycle, so I can drive to the park and go biking. That's my *interest*.

A smart car salesperson will winkle out of me what I really want out of the car—what my true *interest* is—and start making recommendations aimed at my real desire. I might drive out of the showroom in a two-door, zippy coupe with a trunk rack that is more expensive than the original four-door I was looking at. Still, the salesperson has satisfied my desire and their interest in a higher commission.

Principled negotiators generate several options that could potentially satisfy both parties, rather than argue about one option that would clearly favor one side over the other. They make the agreement based on objective reasons and not a desire to please another or crush the competition.

They understand the other party's **Best Alternative To a Negotiated Agreement (BATNA)**. In other words, if you can't reach an agreement, what is the best thing they can do instead? Similarly, you would also know your best alternative if you had to walk away, and you improve it if you can.

Life is not pie; more for one person does not have to mean less for another. In many negotiations, people tend to assume that they would either win or lose, which are the only two options. However, there's often another.

The third alternative is a win-win, where the solution would benefit both parties. It may be harder to find and require more discussion and potentially more time brainstorming the issue. If a win-win cannot be found, the next best thing would be a compromise, where the loss is made as small as possible and distributed evenly.

Stages of Negotiation

Typically, there are five stages to the agreement.

1. Decide to negotiate

First, identify the problem, with negotiation as its solution. You may not want to negotiate every issue; remember the importance of picking your battles.

2. Prepare

There are things you'll need to know before sitting down at the table with your fellow negotiators. Understand the problem itself and your goals for the solution. Are you trying to solve for low costs? What is the ideal outcome for your team?

If you have others supporting you during the process, ensure everyone's roles and responsibilities are clear.

It's crucial to know your own BATNA. If the other side won't give in, or for whatever reason you need to walk away, know what you'll do instead. In the car example, if that salesperson cannot give you what you want, you'll just have to go to a different dealership.

Strengthen yours if you can, then you know you won't agree to anything out of desperation because your BATNA is still a good alternative. It gives you more leverage.

By the same token, understand what the other side's BATNA is and find arguments to make it appear worse if you can. If they need to make the agreement with you, because their alternative is much worse, you've given yourself more leverage.

3. Negotiate

For a successful negotiation, find a third alternative that's ideally a win-win for all parties involved. You'll probably need to brainstorm additional options for everyone to choose from or modify into a win-win.

This stage often requires time and patience. If you cannot get what you want right away, that doesn't mean you should bring a halt to the negotiations. If your BATNA leaves you free to walk away, use that leverage to keep the others at the table.

Once everyone has accepted a specific option, make sure it is captured in writing. Verify that everyone has agreed—especially if someone has remained silent. They may have reservations about it that could cause them to ignore any eventual action plan.

Develop a plan outlining what each party will do with the timeframe and make sure it's clear who would do what. Build in compliance with the written plan, so everyone knows how they'll demonstrate that they kept to the agreement.

4. Implement

Make sure you congratulate everyone for a successful negotiation without gloating; you don't want to burn your bridges. In today's world, people's paths can cross multiple times. Don't make enemies when you don't need to.

Then, the plan needs to be carried out as agreed by all parties.

5. Follow-up

Nurture the relationships you've made. If you could reach a win-win, the parties should then be willing to fulfill promises.

Monitor to make sure all parties are abiding by the agreement.

Guidelines for Successful Negotiations

Although each negotiation is different, there are common elements to those that successfully achieve the parties' goals and result in a win-win. Learning how to interact with others without either acquiescing or becoming too assertive is something that you can practice in everyday life, not to mention the projects you're leading.

- **Three Ps: be prepared, positive, and patient**

    Avoid being caught by surprise, knowing how processes could go wrong or take too long. Prepare; have contingency and risk management plans in place. Ensure that you gather information from everyone involved to understand fully how alternative agreements might impact the work.

    People find it easy to deal with the people they like, so when you bring a positive attitude, your negotiation partners will be more positive in their interactions with you too.

When it comes to negotiations, you need to be patient. Sometimes, you may feel like shutting it down or moving on to something that isn't so uncomfortable. Resist these urges. Take time to answer questions about how a proposed new process would work or allow the other party to think through the implications of the option you offered them.

Likewise, make sure you take time to comprehend their offer and its consequences, along with any second and third-order consequences that could arise.

- **Know your opening offer and your bottom line**

    This aligns with being prepared. Give yourself some room to negotiate rather than starting with your bottom line.

    For example, if you think the project will take between four to six months, don't open with four months or fewer. The other side could ask for three months, and you won't have room to adjust.

    When you have limits, you'll know when it's time to walk away. If you can't run the project on less than $1 million, that's your bottom line. Rebuff any efforts to drop below the million and walk away if they cannot work with that. This also implies that your opening offer must be higher than $1 million, so you can have the room to negotiate.

- **Offer some trial balloons**

    Until the agreement is signed, you won't have to consider anything as final and binding. Make some suggestions. What if the team could address one feature as Phase One, then work on building additional features in later stages, which would allow you to stay at the $1 million mark?

- **Understand your status**

  As the project manager, you would naturally have a significant status because of your proximity to the project. You may well have more than the other party which you should leverage. You could obtain additional concessions if the other side needs to reach an agreement with you.

- **Consider authority**

  You want to deal with the person who has the authority to make decisions on the other side. Dealing with them directly often means you can reach an agreement quicker.

  Conversely, you may want to send a representative out to negotiate on your behalf. You will have time to review the proposal instead of being pressured into an agreement on the spot, and can counter them where necessary.

- **Don't reward intimidation**

  Set expectations and boundaries; don't let other parties push you back over these lines. You'll probably need to learn how to push back against clients who are unreasonable in terms of scope, budget, time, or all three at once. Once you start allowing them to cross the lines, you're training them to continue to do that. Hold the line.

Achieve More with Negotiation

If you want to improve your negotiation techniques, there are some advanced ones you can use. One characteristic of a good negotiator is having a high level of *emotional intelligence*. Rather than being caught up in the emotions—especially during a stressful negotiation—you can focus on interests rather than positions.

Consider improving the following techniques:

- **Use humor**

    Caveat: if you have a dry or dark sense of humor, this strategy may not work well! However, if you can break the ice and get some smiles out of everyone, you can help them relax. It may lead people to back off the cliff and reconsider their stance.

- **Make the pie bigger**

    This is how you would get to the third win-win alternative. Show the people you're negotiating with that your proposal means everyone gets more. If their goal is to maximize benefits from a deal, they can receive even more from your solution than if they won with their proposal.

- **Don't be afraid to show your strength**

    Negotiation isn't gambling; it's not necessarily a bad idea to be open and show your cards. If you're operating from a position of strength because you have a strong BATNA, they'll stay at the table longer to keep you from walking away, assuming theirs is weaker.

    Plus, if they've prepared as you have, they should know your BATNA and be aware of your strength anyway.

- **Take a break when you need to**

    Sometimes, the right thing to do is call a temporary halt. That doesn't mean the negotiation is over, but it's a good idea to let everyone cool off. Otherwise, you may want some time to process an offer or just go to the bathroom. The point is that you don't have to *literally* sit at the negotiating table until you reach the written agreement.

- **Don't fill the silence**

    This tip is particularly powerful after you've made your proposal. Don't rush to justify, rationalize, or explain; let it sit.

Let them look skeptical and be skeptical while they're chewing it over. You don't have to jump in, and you'll look stronger for being able to sit through the silence.

- **Reframe**

    Try to focus on one or two interests and continue to reframe the conversation around them. Doing so keeps it simple and everyone on track. Make sure you have your goals prepared and continue to bring the discussion back when it meanders. Also, keep the conversation around topics where you would have a higher power.

- **Listen actively**

    Be curious about your negotiation partners. Try to get to know them and their thought processes. Concentrate on what they're saying. You can ask questions to clarify and summarize, which can be used as a mini-close.

    Learn where you share interests; you can use them to build an agreement and show that you're not so far apart that you cannot find a third alternative that will leave both of you better off.

- **Tune into station WII-FM**

    This comes into play a lot as a project leader, doesn't it? In a negotiation, you need to know how your offer will benefit the other party. If it doesn't have value to them, why would they agree to it?

- **Understand all sides**

    To reach your goals, you need to know what they are. If you're not already sure what you want out of the process, spend some time figuring that out before you begin negotiating.

    Know what the others want as well. Is there anything that's not important to you that you could use as a tradeoff to get something you do want? Understand that going in as well. You might try to discover what's not as important to them, so you'll know how they're using their leverage. What are their interests? What is their BATNA? What is the acceptable minimum?

Facilitation

This is similar to negotiation, in that you are trying to bring something to a successful close. In this case, it may be a meeting or discussion. Empowering your team means discussions, which might be contentious. Ideally, the facilitator is neutral, but that won't always be possible on projects for PMs because you have a significant stake in the outcome.

There are six core competencies to be a successful coordinator in these situations (Adams et al., 2006).[21]

1. Create collaborative relationships with clients

PMs must develop working and fruitful partnerships with their clients.

2. Develop and maintain a participatory environment

This skill comes along with being a high EQ leader. The project leader must demonstrate openness and humility that encourages everyone to participate. They have to manage conflict and promote the creativity of the team members.

3. Plan good group processes

Not only does a PM need to set aside time and a location for the group to collaborate, but also to choose the methods that would foster an inclusive atmosphere and result in high-quality deliverables.

4. Model professional positivity

Project managers need to act with integrity and trust that the group will find their way.

5. Guide the group to a good outcome

This one is pretty self-explanatory. The group needs to reach a consensus on the subject under discussion, and the PM helps to facilitate that.

6. Develop and sustain knowledge of facilitation

Unlike professional facilitators, project managers don't need to achieve certifications in the field and maintain their professional standing in it. However, they should be aware of the vital facilitation methods that would help them achieve their goals.

Facilitate Effective Discussions

As a facilitator, you'll be guiding the team rather than directing it. One of your main tasks will be to keep the discussion on track and target, and there are several ways you can do that.

- **Use agendas and objectives**

    These provide roadmaps for meetings and can help guide discussions. If there's a problem to be solved on the agenda, it's much easier for everyone to focus on it. When the discussion strays, remind everyone that they need to have a solution by the end of the meeting.

- **List action items and their owners**

    To ensure that nothing is left out, you or a notetaker must capture the plan and everyone's responsibilities.

- **Park tangents in the parking lot**

  As you know, it's incredibly easy for a discussion to go off track! People may bring up important issues that need meetings or action plans of their own, so put them on their own list. The ones who brought up the point can see that it won't be ignored forever, which would help them let go of it during the current discussion.

- **Set ground rules**

  Another theme you've probably noticed as you read through the book is the idea of clarity. It's also essential in a meeting to be clear about whatever rules you set forth.

  Maybe one rule is that everyone puts their cellphone in a basket in the middle of the table. Perhaps there's a topic that needs to be hashed out separately or has already been discussed extensively, which you should ask the participants to avoid so they can concentrate on the actual issue.

- **Set time limits (timeboxing)**

  One way to motivate people to come to a conclusion is to tell them they have five minutes to resolve an issue; then the discussion would move on. This helps those who argue for the fun of it to stop doing so and let the team make a decision.

- **Capture ideas and comments as they come up**

  Discussions move fast. Don't assume you'll have time to go back and ask questions because you won't. Capture everything and ask questions if you didn't hear something or still need clarification. It's good to have a notetaker for this task, so you can focus on the discussion and check the notes after the meetings.

Key Takeaways

Facilitation and negotiation are essential skills that a leader must have to complete a project successfully.

- Negotiation is a complex skill requiring several capabilities. It typically takes place in five stages.
- If you're not a good negotiator now, there will be many ways to improve.
- Facilitation empowers your team members to lead meetings and discussions, and you may need to build these skills as well.

In the next chapter, you will learn about the power of service in leadership.

---

[20] https://www.pmi.org/learning/library/negotiating-project-outcomes-develop-skills-6781
[21] https://www.pmi.org/learning/library/project-meeting-facilitator-more-effective-7988

CHAPTER 7

SERVE FOR SUCCESS

WE'VE talked a lot about how the command-and-control leadership style isn't used much anymore because it's ineffective. You may have heard of *servant leadership*, where the one who's running the show would consider themselves a servant of those who follow them. The idea is that, by understanding the needs of their followers and empowering them, the leader can accomplish more. Followers are motivated and engaged and believe that their needs are taken into consideration.

Being skilled at listening and having a high level of emotional intelligence, including empathy, are crucial for making everything work.

Active Listening

Listening requires concentration and freedom from distractions, yet so many of us claim to be having conversations with others while we hold our cellphones, alert for any buzz or beep that tells us we have a new email or social media notification.

People believe they can multitask—or listen to what the person is saying and check their email at the same time—but that's far from true. The mind switches rapidly between tasks because it cannot conduct them simultaneously (Hamilton, 2008).[22] This rapid switching fatigues your brain. Not only that, but it means you're missing what the other person is saying. Put your phone away when you're talking to someone and be in the moment with them.

Listen to understand what the other person is saying because you need to know what their problem is. They may be complaining about another team member not pulling their weight, but the real issue could be that they feel overwhelmed by all the work they have to do.

Recall that most of the message is nonverbal. While you're listening to the language they use, also recognize the tone and *body language*. Sometimes, they may be saying one thing, but their tone and nonverbal communication may suggest another. Asking questions will help you get to the bottom of the matter.

"Seek first to understand, then to be understood." —Stephen Covey

When you want to solve a problem, you have to listen first. When someone's talking to you, how would you know their problem if you don't pay attention? If you assume you know what it is because it sounds like a problem you've heard before, your solution won't work.

You didn't define the problem correctly, because you didn't listen to the person actively. If you don't think you understand what they mean, ask more questions and clarify until you can summarize it and they confirm that's the problem.

About 75-90% of a project manager's time is spent in communication (Haus, 2016).[23] Don't worry; we'll get to that topic in more detail in the next chapter. However, that doesn't mean you should be spending all that time talking; you have two ears and one mouth for a reason. Fortunately, active listening is something you can practice anywhere—not just at the worksite. Practice putting your phone down and listening to what your kids, spouse, and friends want to say. You might be surprised how interesting they are when you're not distracted.

Emotional intelligence (EQ)

It's always been important for leaders to have a decent IQ, which measures critical thinking skills. But today's modern business world demands a high EQ as well. When managed effectively, emotions help build interpersonal relationships and create strong bonds that so many people are searching for. It's much more fun and easy to work on a project that you love than one where you're just going through the motions.

You might remember that there are four aspects to emotional intelligence that allow you to develop the environment your team members—and even stakeholders—can thrive in. The good news is that EQ—unlike IQ—is not fixed, and you can work on improving yours.

1. Self-awareness

This includes recognizing and understanding one's own emotions. Build this skill by:

- Naming the emotion.
- Journaling about it.
- Letting your body alert you—for example, many people find their stomach tightening when they're stressed.

2. Emotional management

This is where you would think before you react based on your emotions, as expressing them may be inappropriate at certain times. Build this skill by:

- Taking responsibility for your own life without playing the victim or blaming others.
- Pausing before speaking and asking yourself if what you're about to say is necessary, kind, and true.
- Requesting feedback.
- Finding humor in the situation.

3. Self-motivation

Build this skill by:

- Visualizing success.
- Networking with like-minded people.
- Using positive affirmations.

4. Management of others' emotions

This is also helping them regulate their emotions, so they can be productive. Build this skill by:

- Putting yourself in the other person's shoes.
- Listening without judging or problem solving.
- Modeling how you want others to behave by demonstrating the behavior yourself.

You must start by managing your own emotions before you can move on to helping others. It's like being on an airplane: when the oxygen masks come down, you would put yours on first. That's what enables you to help others.

There are many benefits of having a high EQ as a project leader, particularly in terms of relationships. That would include not only the people on your team but also the client and stakeholders. By understanding your emotions, you give others the space to accept theirs. You'll also accept other people as they are, which will help them to bond with you.

When you can recognize your character and the fact that you make mistakes, it becomes easier for team members to hold themselves accountable for their work. Being open and emotionally honest as the PM gives everyone else the confidence to be honest as well, which is what you need for a well-functioning team unit.

Problem solving relies on all team members being comfortable enough to challenge others and voice their ideas. They need the psychological space to do so, which you can provide as a leader with high EQ. Those who know they won't be shamed for making mistakes or raising unpopular opinions can feel free to brainstorm and own their responsibilities.

Empathy

This is a critical component of having high emotional intelligence: not sympathy, but empathy. Both are useful, but empathy is more important to a PM. Sympathy is when you feel sorry for someone else's misfortune. If the father of one of your team members dies, you would feel sympathy for them.

Sometimes people believe mistakenly that empathy is merely stepping into someone else's shoes, but you're still looking out at the world from your own perspective. Empathy is actually perceiving the world the way someone else would see it—someone with a background, educational achievement, and experiences that are different from yours. This is much harder but more rewarding.

Once you realize where someone's coming from, you can understand better why they're not as enthusiastic about the project as you are, or why they're having more difficulty with something than you had anticipated. It's not a personal vendetta against you or a desire to throw a wrench into the works.

All team members have a life outside of work, as do you hopefully! Such also implies that there will be issues affecting their work in one way or another. As a PM, you must be aware of these, and when you've built connections with team members, they'll let you know what's happening.

There may be times when you need to cut them a break. People aren't robots, and no one can expect them to behave like automatons. An empathetic project leader will understand what's happening and adjust expectations accordingly.

Key Takeaways

Serving your followers is a critical factor in success with modern projects. A project leader with high emotional intelligence is best able to lead their team and have the members motivated and determined enough to achieve their goals.

- Active listening is a critical skill that all PMs need to master, knowing that they must understand the other person first before they can begin to offer solutions.

- High emotional intelligence can be developed and is essential for building relationships with team members, clients, and stakeholders.

- Empathy is a crucial factor in emotional intelligence, and it allows you to see the world from someone else's viewpoint.

In the next chapter, you will learn how to improve your communication.

---

[22] https://www.npr.org/templates/story/story.php?storyId=95256794
[23] https://www.projectmanagement.com/blog-post/18979/Are-Your-Communication-Habits-Good-Enough-

CHAPTER 8

WHAT WE HAVE HERE IS A FAILURE TO COMMUNICATE

WE learn to talk at an early age. Usually, we would start off by making demands, and as we grow older, we develop the ability to hold a conversation. As a project manager, you might have developed some decent communication skills. However, no matter what your starting point is, you can always improve.

Communication seems very simple since most of us have been doing it pretty much our entire lives. We listen when someone else speaks, and when we talk, other people listen—at least in theory. But if it's so easy, why is one of the most common complaints about work life the *lack* of communication?

This topic is particularly critical for project managers because you are the nexus between the client, team, and stakeholders. As a project leader, you need to influence and persuade senior management to endorse and promote the project, get the resources you need from line management, and generate stakeholder support as well. If your communication skills aren't tip-top, you could endanger your own success.

I've led several different projects and initiatives, and I'll tell you the two absolutely necessary elements for being a leader; one is the ability to gather information and understand the situation of the past, where it is now, and where it will be in the future once you have achieved your goals.

The second is to distribute this information clearly and convincingly. Remember that whether you think you can achieve the goal or you cannot, you're right. Everyone around you must understand precisely what you're trying to tell them and believe that you believe it can be done.

Process of Communication

The procedure for interacting with others is simple, which doesn't mean that getting your exact message across will always be easy. There's a sender and a receiver of the message, which may be delivered through different media, such as emails, face-to-face conversations, or online forums.

When you're the receiver, you should be practicing active listening skills, as discussed earlier. Summarize when you think you understand and ask questions when you don't. Once you have agreement from the other person that your summary is exactly what they're trying to get across, you know you haven't misinterpreted anything and can move on.

When you are the sender of the message, though, there's no guarantee that the other person is actively listening to you. They may be waiting for you to hurry up and finish so they can jump in, or they've been distracted by their cell phone, so they only heard about half of what you were talking about or misunderstood your message.

The context of your message may affect how the other person perceives it. For example, a stakeholder could interpret your words differently from how a team member would. Either of them could interpret your words differently if they experienced a positive life event recently, like getting married, or a negative one like getting divorced. In other words, there are a variety of reasons why your message won't be copied from your thoughts to what the other person understands.

Face-to-face communication contains a lot more information than any other method of transmission. Because digital messages are more limited, they're more likely to be misunderstood. However, you are accountable for the project's results, so it would be in your best interest to ensure that your message is delivered as clearly as possible to minimize misinterpretations, even if the people receiving the message aren't using good listening techniques.

Expectations

One reason why messages could fail is if you don't set expectations. With your project team members, you would set the rules for what would be appropriate. There may be some guidelines that you can expect them to follow absolutely, but for the rest, empower them to get everything done as they see fit.

When you have a team of high achievers, you'll want to reduce the amount of work where you have a procedure for them to follow. Be humble and recognize that they might have a faster or better solution than yours. Consider breaking up large tasks into smaller pieces. Whenever a little goal is achieved, the team member can check off a box and see how far they've progressed.

You need to set expectations with other stakeholders, such as clients and vendors. How often would you sit down for a meeting? Some may be all too eager to block off time on their calendars, whereas others may require your persuasion skills to set regular update meetings. How will they get messages to you and the team? Again, make sure any boundaries or guidelines you're setting are clear, precise, and agreed to with the other party.

Influencing and Persuasion

As a high EQ leader, you already know that you cannot command your project team members like an old-school general. You also understand that you cannot mistreat the client or order them around. For all the people you have relationships with on the project, there will probably be times when you need to convert them to your way of thinking. These are skills that you can develop through practice, both at work and in your personal life. There are several ways to increase your influence as a project manager.

- **Let go of the result**

    Don't spend so much time worrying about whether you'll achieve your goal with communication. You don't have control over whether someone else agrees with you or not. You have control over your message.

    What are the benefits of your suggestion for the other person's organization and for them personally? Take your time exploring that instead.

- **Crowdsource with other PMs**

    Ask colleagues how they would or have handled a similar situation, and what kind of results they got. Have them look over your proposal and decide if they have any suggestions.

- **Create multiple proposals**

    In other words, have a Plan B, and maybe also a Plan C if your first idea doesn't go over well. Someone who didn't like your first suggestion could still be amenable to finding a different solution.

- **Question your assumptions**

    Ask yourself what you're assuming about the person you want to speak with. Are those assumptions valid? Before you make a proposal based on the assumption, ensure that it's right first.

- **Find your weakest link**

    What is the weakest aspect of your proposal? Once you've identified it, see if there's a way you can make it stronger.

- **Always act with integrity**

    As soon as people perceive you as dishonest or acting with a hidden agenda, they will lose trust in you. If they don't trust you, they won't be influenced by you, no matter how much of a smooth talker you are.

Stakeholders

One key communication channel that you will have while on a project is with the stakeholders. You need to keep them apprised of what's going on and enlist their help in various ways to deliver the project successfully. You'll often find yourself using your powers of persuasion with them.

You might recall that a stakeholder is literally anyone who has a *stake* in the project; anyone who is impacted by it. Stakeholders include clients, project team members, colleagues, managers, executives, and suppliers. They may be within the organization that's sponsoring the project or external, such as vendors and regulatory authorities.

If the project doesn't meet the stakeholders' expectations, it could be considered a failure. You need to keep them all in mind. Sometimes, the needs of one group might clash with another. For example, you might be working on a project to bring a new product to your client's market, but the regulatory authorities have some concerns about it.

This would mean that you need to tailor your message to them individually, so they can have the information they need. For example, your discussions with senior executives or high-level officers will typically be at a 30,000-foot height, giving them the highlights of the progress and challenges. They won't have the time to deal with smaller details and mostly prefer a brief summary rather than an in-depth discussion.

By contrast, your talks with the project team about the same subjects could be lengthy. They would require more details than you have considered, so the team would develop an original way to solve it.

Each interaction with a stakeholder is a chance to improve the relationship. Even if you already have a solid bond, there should be no reason not to make it even stronger.

Effective Communication

This is what supports the ultimate project success. When you're communicating with the wrong people, sending incorrect information, too much, or too little, you're decreasing the chances of achieving your goals. It starts with knowledge—who your stakeholders are, what the client's business objectives are, and how the project aligns with them.

Before you get started putting together the plan, it helps to answer the **Five Ws and an H**: Who, What, When, Where, Why, and How.

- **Who** will you be communicating with? In other words, who are your stakeholders?
- **What** is the message? Will you probably have more than one?
- **When** will the message(s) be sent? Like voting, communication should happen early and often.
- **Where** will the messages be disseminated? Online, in person, or both?
- **Why** do the receivers need the message? Remember to tailor it to the person and tell them what the benefit is for them.
- **How** will the message(s) be sent? Email, online forum, in person, one-on-one, town hall, or all of the above?

For communication to be *effective*, it must be the **right message**, sent at the **right time**, to the **right people**, and in the **right way**.

1. Right people

These are the stakeholders, and a vital function for project success is not only to identify all of them but also to determine WII-FM for each of them.

Match KPIs (key performance indicators) for all levels of management. If they're rewarded based on productivity, calculate how much more productive their teams will be once they've implemented the improvement, for example.

Once you know how the project benefits each stakeholder, you can craft your message appropriately.

2. Right way

For each stakeholder and message, consider the best mode of communication. If you have something that needs to be disseminated quickly across the organization, an email could be the best way to get that information across. Newsletters and intranet are similar possibilities.

If the company has a knowledge repository or central data hub, as a project manager, you need to know how it gets updated and by whom.

There are times when collaboration is called for, especially if a decision must be made. Although email has undoubtedly been used in the past—where participants would go back and forth until they reach a resolution—it's inefficient. Face-to-face or virtual meetings over video calls are best for collaboration.

Know whether messages are being sent internally or externally, and you need to be careful when sending them outside the organization. Include nondisclosure agreements, no confidential or intellectual property, and follow the company's guidelines.

Even for internal communications, not all employees will have the same level of knowledge about specific projects and operations. Be careful about what's considered confidential within the firm.

3. Right message

Consider the person that you're communicating with for each message. What is the appropriate level of detail? Bring your empathy to the message and step into their shoes. It's critical for all stakeholders that you consider the information from their viewpoint.

Does this mean that you must craft a separate email for each person you need to communicate with? That's just not realistic, given all other demands on your time. Think about the groups of people who need to get the message similarly instead.

For example, you may be dealing with executives in different departments, but they all just need a summarized update of what's happening. They can get the same email. Likewise, although your team members are working on different aspects of the project, you can send out one email to all of them with team-specific information.

Templates are also beneficial when you're trying to maximize the time you spend on communications. Have a status report template that you can update and send to all interested parties, for example.

However, not all communication can be satisfied with emails and templates sent to everyone. Sometimes—and especially when you're working with large and mature firms—there will be a central hub where you can keep updates and other information instead.

The key to successful and clear communication is keeping it short and straightforward. No one has the time to read a wall of text these days, so don't send one. Keep your missive objective short, focused on the project, and containing what you want people to know.

When you need to share bad news, don't try to hide it in a thicket of sentences or irrelevant information. Be clear about it and offer solutions without excusing or blaming.

What action do you want the receiver to take upon from the message? If you have a call to action, make it clear what the recipient is intended to do and don't bury it in a tangle or irrelevance either. You may want to separate it visually from the rest of the message to draw their attention to it.

4. Right time

Communication must be frequent so that everyone can have the latest information. You may discuss with your stakeholders how often it would be reasonable for them to hear from you. Be prepared and propose a frequency because stakeholders often rely on you being an expert who knows what's best.

Don't let them demand too much communication that could interfere with the project. On the other hand, monthly or quarterly meetings are not frequent enough when you have decisions to be made weekly.

Automation works well for regular messages, and many project management software applications contain this functionality. In addition to timed messages that occur regularly, you'll also need to deliver them on a more ad-hoc basis, especially in times of crisis or emergency.

How Effective is Your Communication?

It's helpful to measure whether you're getting your message across, so you can fine-tune anything that needs to be adjusted. As a PM, you're not the most objective assessor of the impact of your messages; therefore, you need to ask the recipients for feedback.

- **Regularly**

    When you set the expectation that you want to receive constructive criticism on your communication skills, so you can serve your stakeholders more professionally, it helps them feel better about providing that feedback.

    Feedback isn't a one-and-done type of deal; it should be a loop where you would ask for feedback, receive it, incorporate it, and ask for it again.

- **Ask during meetings**

    Whether in a meeting with your team or one-on-one, you can ask if they're getting the information they need for their job. How can your communication be improved? Is there anything they like or want you to do more of?

- **Ask in your written messages**

    In your emails, you can ask specifically if there is more information they need to make a decision to be more effective in their jobs.

- **Anonymous surveys**

    Sometimes, people are a little reluctant to give direct feedback because it makes them feel like they're attacking the other person, even when they're not. Likewise, people may just be unwilling to give you feedback, especially if you are still working on this aspect of your leadership and tend to get defensive. An anonymous online survey is the easiest way to gather feedback if your requests aren't providing useful information. They're easy to set up, and you can give everyone space to write comments.

- **Listen**

    When people provide feedback, you may want to rationalize, excuse, justify, or blame someone else. Do none of the above. Practice your active listening skills and only speak to clarify or summarize, so you can ensure you understand what they're telling you. Be humble.

Don't forget to incorporate that feedback and let everyone know! You can ask for feedback as much as you want, but if people think you're ignoring it, they won't want to waste their time any longer. Once you have gathered the feedback, implement it. Then, let the stakeholders know what you've done to incorporate what they suggested.

Key Takeaways

In real estate, they always say it's about location, location, location. But in project management, it's about communication, communication, communication.

- There's a communication process that involves the sender, receiver, and message, though it ends up being more complex than that.

- You need to set clear and reasonable expectations for team members and stakeholders.

- PMs must develop their influence and persuasion skills to increase the chances for project success.

- Effective communication involves sending the right **message** at the right **time** in the right **way** to the right **people**.

- Ask for feedback to improve your communication.

In the next chapter, you will learn about essential leadership traits that all PMs must have.

CHAPTER 9

HECG SECRET FOR SUCCESS

AS they used to say in the old TV commercials: *but wait! There's more!* Yes, we have discussed many topics, characteristics, skills, and information that a successful project manager needs to know. However, there are still a handful more, and mastering them will put you on the road to becoming the kind of a leader that you've always wanted to be.

Humility

We've touched on this trait briefly, especially in the section about emotional intelligence. By now, you know that it's necessary to create an open and honest environment that will help you get most out of your project team. When the team leader is humble and admits they don't know everything, it creates space for them and others to make mistakes and learn from them.

You've also discovered that a key factor in leadership is continuous learning and improvement. By definition, if you think you know everything already, you block yourself from learning; if you can't learn, you can't improve. No one human being could possibly know everything there is to comprehend; one look at the Internet can tell you that.

It's essential that you understand what you don't know. Although this is the third book I've written about the various aspects of project management, you can see that there is still more to learn. However, now you have a thorough grounding in the fundamentals and can be confident about going out and building on this new base of knowledge.

You may have heard of the Dunning-Kruger effect or the Dunning-Kruger experiment. Two researchers—David Dunning and Justin Kruger—discovered that people who are incompetent at something generally think they're much greater than they are. Contrarily, those who are actually competent at the same thing usually believe they are less capable than they truly are (Murphy, 2017).[24] This is partially due to humility because competent people understand how much they *don't know* about the chosen topic. You don't want anyone to call you a walking Dunning-Kruger effect because that means you behave like you're much more competent than you actually are!

Other common issues for project managers who aren't appropriately humble include taking unnecessary risks or not planning adequately because they believe they can figure everything out. In this case, they would be focusing on themselves rather than the team or project, not involving enough people in collaboration activities, and concentrating on reputation instead of work or shared values. You probably recognize already that these issues are antithetical to project success and leadership in general.

There are a number of ways you can demonstrate humility and increase the chances for project success at the same time. You can nurture the humble side of your nature as you go through life.

- **Take responsibility**

    Giving up responsibility means losing the power to change the future because the power is given to other people or circumstances; thus, success becomes a matter of sheer luck. You're the one in charge of your life, and humble people own it.

- **Admit when you don't know**

    You know that humility is important and that no one person understands everything about the world. Therefore, admitting that you don't know something is not a badge of shame, but a recognition of reality.

- **Listen and respect others' ideas**

    It's not enough to listen actively, although that is an excellent first step. You also need to avoid dismissing other people's ideas outright. Wouldn't you want to use a great idea to make sure the project is successful, even if it isn't your idea?

- **Show care for your team**

    For a humble leader, followers are valuable, so take care of your team members.

- **Appreciate others' work**

    You might be frugal with your budget, but it's a bad idea to be frugal with praise. If a team member does well, celebrate it. Praise those who make an effort and take time to appreciate everyone's contributions to the project.

- **Be flexible**

    Not only is using agile methodology a good idea but so is being agile with your decisions! Roll with the punches, so your team members can adapt too.

- **Don't micromanage**

    We've discussed how wasteful and unnecessary micromanagement is, and here's another way to look at it: when you're hovering over your team like a helicopter, you're basically telling them you know better than they do, so they must do everything your way.

- **Reflect and improve**

    Even if you are a project manager, you're still human! You'll make mistakes, just as your team will. Take time to look back periodically and think about what went well and what didn't. Use that information to make things better.

Enthusiasm

Consider the people you follow—your mentors or even famous figures that you want to emulate. Are they passionate about what they do? Are they eager to share their knowledge with others? Or are they noncommittal when they talk about what they do?

Right. You want to follow someone who's enthusiastic about their life and the path they've taken. To model this for your team and the other stakeholders, you'll need to discover your motivators.

External motivators like money work for a while, but not for as long as you may think. You'll need to find personal motivation to continue when things get tough. Pride in your work? The satisfaction of tackling a difficult challenge and emerging victorious? Gratification from developing team members into the best people they can be? Feel free to choose more than one and write them down, so you can refer back when times are hard.

Other ways to maintain enthusiasm include getting involved in project management as a profession by giving lectures or teaching. Change things up by volunteering for other projects, either at home or at work. Let go of the things you can't control, so you can focus your energy where you can make a difference.

Composure

As they say, *"Keep calm and carry on."*[25] Projects have a tendency to generate chaos. The larger and more complex—and the more stakeholders you have—the easier it will be for things to spin out of control.

However, as the project leader, you need to stay cool when everything's heating up around you. Model a matter-of-fact approach to problems for your team members and other stakeholders. No matter how much pressure you experience, resist the temptation to dump it onto others' shoulders, particularly your project team.

Another way to handle stress in addition to what was mentioned in Chapter One is to reframe your idea of stress into one of opportunity. Situations that bring additional pressure are often the same ones that would allow you to grow and develop as a person and PM. Look at these events as challenges, where you would have a chance to influence the outcome, then get to problem solving.

Guide

You now know that being a leader also includes being part of the team. You can also think about project leadership as being a guide. Imagine that you're a sherpa taking a group of well-equipped travelers up the mountain. You wouldn't tell them where to put their feet exactly, but you would take them on the trails that you're familiar with. When you get to a fork, you allow travelers to decide which way to go, but you would provide them with your recommendation and the pros and cons of each path if they can't find them.

Sometimes, you will come across a boulder that wasn't in the path before. You clear it away for them or steer them in a path around it. There will be times when the travelers argue about which way to go, and you would be the voice of reason to help them get back to thinking logically through the problem.

When the trail is steep, you would be the one encouraging and motivating everyone to keep going. There will still be times when you need to make an executive decision because the group cannot agree or doesn't have the expertise on the mountain that you do. I think you can see how this fits into your abilities as a project manager.

Key Takeaways

The icing on the project manager sundae is HECG for success: Humility, Enthusiasm, Composure, and Guide.

- Being humble is vital for admitting to your mistakes and learning from those around you, so you can be more successful as a PM.

- People want to follow leaders who are enthusiastic about what they do.

- Stay calm, cool, and collected to help those around you avoid getting caught up in the chaos.

- PMs act as guides for all stakeholders and team members in a project.

---

[24] https://www.forbes.com/sites/markmurphy/2017/01/24/the-dunning-kruger-effect-shows-why-some-people-think-theyre-great-even-when-their-work-is-terrible/#1a8d1f995d7c

[25] https://www.keepcalmandcarryon.com/history/

FINAL WORDS

NOW that you've read through this book, you should have a solid grasp of the kinds of leadership skills that will help you become not just a successful project manager, but also a person with high emotional intelligence. The modern leader empowers and motivates their team members and develops them too.

In previous books, we talked more about the technical skills of project management; but in this one, we focused on leadership, which is almost exclusively about the people. There are various traits that good leaders must have to bring out the best in everyone involved in the project to a successful conclusion and how to deal with common interpersonal problems that arise frequently.

There are many characteristics and skills for a PM to be a successful leader, increasing their ability to become a successful project leader. Problem solving is a key capability, especially when it comes to dealing with issues like politics.

Another crucial skill is conflict management. When you have two or more people in a room or working on a project together, there will be disagreements. Some disagreement is constructive; however, conflicts based on personalities and relationships are typically unhealthy, and the PM needs to work through and eliminate them.

Teams need building and managing. Project managers are responsible for holding the team together through the phases of team building (forming, storming, norming, performing, and adjourning) and hopefully reaching the performing stage, where the team would be acting as a cohesive unit.

Beyond managing the team well, a good project leader will also help develop individual members. This can be done through coaching or mentoring, which is a longer-term process that assists the mentee in developing their career. PMs must understand the people and cultures on their team and delegate to help them grow by taking more challenging assignments.

Negotiation is a life skill that's also particularly critical for project managers. They need to be capable facilitators to help others run meetings and workshops while staying on track.

The idea of servant leadership—or having the leader serve their followers—has grown recently in popularity. To do this properly, the project manager must listen actively and demonstrate high EQ, including empathy, instead of sympathy.

Communication is the lifeblood of any successful project. Being clear and getting one's message across to stakeholders and team members is key to achieving project goals. Communication does involve not only the sender of the message, but also the receiver. PMs need to use their powers of influence and persuasion.

Effective communication involves sending the right message in the right way to the right people at the right time. Project managers can determine whether their communication is effective by requesting feedback. Finally, great project leaders act as guides to everyone involved in the project, demonstrate humility and enthusiasm, and stay calm under pressure.

If you can take only one message away from this book, I hope it's that although there are numerous skills involved in being a leader, all of them can be developed and improved with deliberate practice.

You have everything you need to know to be a *great project leader*. The more you develop your leadership capabilities, the better off you will be in all areas of life. Don't be afraid to make mistakes; just make sure you own and take responsibility for them.

Take everything that you've learned and use it to help you launch a career as a fabulously successful project manager. It's time for you to soar!

LEAVE A REVIEW

I would be incredibly *thankful* if you could take just 60 seconds to write a brief review on Amazon, even if it's just a few sentences.

If you have downloaded the *Negotiation* checklist (the link is at the beginning of the book), you can attach it to your review and share your experience. Most people struggle with negotiation, and the tips and techniques summarized on the checklist will help you to improve and have more courage.

Please type this link into your browser or scan the QR code:
amazon.com/dp/B08Q4LLB7L

Customer Reviews

★★★★★ 51
4.8 out of 5 stars ▼

5 star	▬▬▬▬▬▬	94%
4 star	▬	2%
3 star		0%
2 star	▬	2%
1 star	▬	2%

See all 51 customer reviews ▸

Share your thoughts with other customers

[Write a customer review]

My Other Books You Will Love

 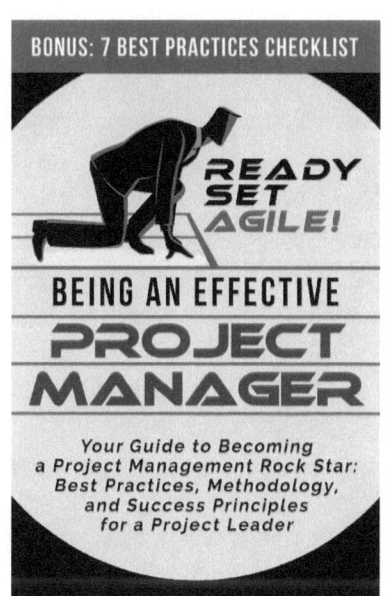

For a complete collection of books, visit the author page
amazon.com/author/rsagile

REFERENCES

Adams, T., & Means, J. (2006). **The project meeting facilitator.** Project Management Institute. https://www.pmi.org/learning/library/project-meeting-facilitator-more-effective-7988

ASQ. (n.d.). **What is a Fishbone Diagram? Ishikawa Cause & Effect Diagram.** Retrieved from https://asq.org/quality-resources/fishbone

Casper, C. M. (2002). **Using emotional intelligence to improve project performance.** Project Management Institute. https://www.pmi.org/learning/library/emotional-intelligence-improve-project-performance-1019

Center for Creative Leadership. (2020, April 28). **Use Active Listening Skills When Coaching Others.** Retrieved from https://www.ccl.org/articles/leading-effectively-articles/coaching-others-use-active-listening-skills/

Clark, T. (2019, November 11). **9 Tips to Become a More Effective Delegator.** LiquidPlanner. https://www.liquidplanner.com/blog/9-tips-become-effective-delegator/

Cooper, A. (2020, June 23). **Building Your Project Team.** Project Smart. https://www.projectsmart.co.uk/building-your-project-team.php

Covey, S. R. (2013). **The 7 Habits of Highly Effective People: Powerful Lessons in Personal Change.** (Anniversary ed.). Simon & Schuster.

D'Amico, J. (2017, December 7). **Project Management Training Tips: Methods of Persuasion.** American Management Association. https://playbook.amanet.org/training-articles-project-management-tips-persuasion/

Daskal, L. (2018, June 10). **7 Powerful Habits That Make You More Assertive.** Retrieved from https://www.lollydaskal.com/leadership/7-powerful-habits-that-make-you-more-assertive/

Economy, P. (2020, February 6). **5 Remarkably Powerful Ways to Boost Your Confidence.** Retrieved from https://www.inc.com/peter-economy/5-remarkably-powerful-ways-to-boost-your-confidence.html

Englund, R. (2010). **Negotiating for success.** Project Management Institute. https://www.pmi.org/learning/library/negotiating-project-outcomes-develop-skills-6781

Fastenberg, D. (2010, October 18). **Top 10 Worst Bosses.** TIME http://content.time.com/time/specials/packages/article/0,28804,2025898_2025900_2026107,00.html

Goodrich, B. (2019, November 19). **Develop vs Manage Project Team.** PM Learning Solutions. https://www.pmlearningsolutions.com/blog/develop-versus-manage-project-team-pmp-concept-36

Hamilton, J. (2008, October 2). **Think You're Multitasking? Think Again.** NPR. https://choice.npr.org/index.html?origin=https://www.npr.org/templates/story/story.php?storyId=95256794

Harvard Professional Development. (2019, August 26). **How to Improve Your Emotional Intelligence.** Retrieved from https://blog.dce.harvard.edu/professional-development/how-improve-your-emotional-intelligence

Henderson, L. (2018, June 22). **Why Our Brains See the World as "Us" versus "Them."** Scientific American. https://www.scientificamerican.com/article/why-our-brains-see-the-world-as-us-versus-them/

Ikigai Consulting. (2016, August 31). **Humility And Project Management.** Retrieved from https://www.ikigaiconsulting.com/insights/humility-and-project-management

Irwin, B. (2007). **Politics, Leadership, and the Art of Relating To Your Team.** Project Management Institute. https://www.pmi.org/learning/library/politics-leadership-relating-project-team-7276

Keep Calm and Carry On. (n.d.). **History.** Keep Calm and Carry On. https://www.keepcalmandcarryon.com/history/

Levin, G. (2011). **Mentoring—a key competency for program and project professionals.** Project Management Institute. https://www.pmi.org/learning/library/mentoring-key-competency-program-project-professionals-6264

Miller, C. (2016, February 26). **Are Your Communication Habits Good Enough?** Project Management. https://www.projectmanagement.com/blog-post/18979/Are-Your-Communication-Habits-Good-Enough–

Mind Tools. (n.d.). **Boost Your Interpersonal Skills: Building Highly Effective Working Relationships.** Retrieved from https://www.mindtools.com/pages/article/interpersonal-skills.htm

Mind Tools. (n.d.). **Building Self-Confidence: Preparing Yourself for Success.** Retrieved from https://www.mindtools.com/selfconf.html

Morfin, E. (2000). **New Rules for Effective Problem Solving in Projects.** Project Management Institute. https://www.pmi.org/learning/library/appraisal-situation-problem-solving-projects-492

Murphy, M. (2017, January 24). **The Dunning-Kruger Effect Shows Why Some People Think They're Great Even When Their Work Is Terrible.** Forbes. https://www.forbes.com/sites/markmurphy/2017/01/24/the-dunning-kruger-effect-shows-why-some-people-think-theyre-great-even-when-their-work-is-terrible/#1a8d1f995d7c

Nguyen, T. (2014, November 24). **You Don't Say? Body Language Speaks Volumes More Than Words.** Entrepreneur Europe. https://www.entrepreneur.com/article/239831

Ni, P. (2014, October 5). **How to Increase Your Emotional Intelligence - 6 Essentials.** Psychology Today https://www.psychologytoday.com/us/blog/communication-success/201410/how-increase-your-emotional-intelligence-6-essentials

Obikunle, O. (2002). **Dealing with cultural diversity in project management.** Project Management Institute. https://www.pmi.org/learning/library/dealing-cultural-diversity-project-management-129

Peterka, P. (2019, September 6). **Root Cause Analysis (RCA) for Beginners.** 6Sigma. https://www.6sigma.us/etc/root-cause-analysis-for-beginners/

Planisware. (2020, April 3). **The conflict management guide for project managers.** Retrieved from https://www.planisware.com/hub/blog/conflict-management-guide-project-managers

Project Management Skills. (n.d.). **Problem Solving Techniques & Strategies for Project Managers.** Retrieved from https://www.project-management-skills.com/problem-solving-techniques.html

Psychology Today. (n.d.). **Emotional Intelligence. What Is Emotional Intelligence?** Retrieved from https://www.psychologytoday.com/us/basics/emotional-intelligence

Rajkumar, S. (2010). **Art of communication in project management.** Project Management Institute. https://www.pmi.org/learning/library/effective-communication-better-project-management-6480

Skelsey, D. (n.d.). **10 Most Common Problems In Projects.** Project Laneways. https://www.project-laneways.com.au/blog/articles/10-most-common-problems-in-projects

Stamoulis, D. (n.d.). **Making It To the Top.** Retrieved from https://www.russellreynolds.com/insights/thought-leadership/making-it-to-the-top-nine-attributes-that-differentiate-ceos

Stickney, F., & Johnston, W. (1983). **Delegation and a sharing of authority by the project manager.** Project Management Institute. https://www.pmi.org/learning/library/delegation-sharing-authority-matrix-organizations-1806

Thamhain, H. (2007). **Managing project teams in an age of complexity.** Project Management Institute. https://www.pmi.org/learning/library/managing-project-teams-age-complexity-7212

Toggl. (n.d.). **5 Stages of Team Development.** Retrieved from https://toggl.com/stages-of-team-development/

Villax, C., & Anantatmula, C. (2010). **Understanding and Managing Conflict in a Project Environment.** Project Management Institute. https://www.pmi.org/learning/library/understanding-managing-conflict-resolution-strategies-6484

Wachtel, D. (2020, June 22). **How to Improve Your Negotiation Skills.** Negotiations Experts. https://www.negotiations.com/articles/negotiating-skills/

Wikipedia contributors. (2020, June 29). **Five whys.** Retrieved from https://en.wikipedia.org/wiki/Five_whys

Wikipedia contributors. (2020, June 6). **Trust, but verify.** Retrieved from https://en.wikipedia.org/wiki/Trust,_but_verify

Wilemon, D., & Thamhain, H. (1983). **Team building in project management.** Project Management Institute. https://www.pmi.org/learning/library/team-building-development-project-management-5707

Wilson, F. (2020, April 30). **9 Effective Team Management Techniques for Project Managers.** NTask. https://www.ntaskmanager.com/blog/effective-team-management/

Woods, J., & Abdon, P. (2011). **The project manager as team coach—a plan for success.** Project Management Institute. https://www.pmi.org/learning/library/project-manager-team-coach-plan-success-6251

Wong, J. P. (2007). **Beat the burnout.** Project Management Institute. https://www.pmi.org/learning/library/eight-practices-maintain-project-enthusiasm-4575

GLOSSARY AND ABBREVIATIONS

Active listening: Absorbing what the speaker is saying thoroughly .... ch. 7
Adjourning/mourning: The last stage of a team building .... ch. 4
Assertiveness: Communicating directly and respectfully .... ch. 1
Analysis paralysis: Overthinking; not allowing decision making .... ch. 2
BATNA: Best Alternative To a Negotiated Agreement .... ch. 6
BECC: Bond, Empathize, Connect, and Communicate .... ch. 4
CEO: Chief Executive Officer .... ch. 1
Coachable: A person willing to learn from someone else in a competency .... ch. 5
Coaching: A development method to support in achieving a goal .... ch. 5
Dunning-Kruger effect: Incompetent people think they are great .... ch. 9
EQ: Emotional Intelligence (understanding and managing emotions) .... ch. 7
Emotional Management: Acting rationally, not reacting emotionally .... ch. 7
Empathy: Understanding or feeling what another person is experiencing .... ch. 7
Extrinsic motivators: External motivators, such as salary, bonuses, time off .... ch. 4
Fishbone diagram: Cause and effect or Ishikawa diagram .... ch. 2
Five Ws and an H: Who, What, When, Where, Why, and How .... ch. 8
Five Whys: A root cause analysis framework .... ch. 2
Forming: The first stage of a team building .... ch. 4
Framework: Describes how to achieve a goal following a methodology .... ch. 2
Global project: A project with members in different locations .... ch. 3
Issue log: A list of all issues with their descriptions and statuses .... ch. 4
Intrinsic motivators: Internal motivators, such as being proud, exciting work .... ch. 4
KPIs: Key Performance Indicators .... ch. 8
Leadership: A combination of skills, characteristics, and behaviors .... ch. 1
Mentoring: Guidance by a more experienced person .... ch. 5
Mind Map: Generating and mapping ideas visually .... ch. 2

Nonverbal communication: Tone, speed of speech, body language .... ch. 1
Norming: The third stage of a team building .... ch. 4
Performing: The fourth and desired stage of a team building .... ch. 4
PM: Project Management .... ch. 1
PMI: Project Management Institute .... ch. 2
Sandwich the critique: Positive statements before and after critique .... ch. 4
Self-awareness: Recognizing and understanding their own emotions .... ch. 7
Soft skills: Communication, leadership, and relationship skills .... ch. 5
Stakeholder: Has "stake" in the outcome of the project .... ch. 8
Storming: The second stage of a team building .... ch. 4
Three Ps: Prepared, Positive, and Patient (a negotiation guideline) .... ch. 6
WBS: Work Breakdown Structure (a tree structure with activities) .... ch. 4
WII-FM: What's In It For Me or Them (a way of communication) .... ch. 4

BEING A
PROJECT LEADER

2020

www.ingramcontent.com/pod-product-compliance
Lightning Source LLC
Chambersburg PA
CBHW021446070526
44577CB00002B/275